PEARSON ALWAYS LEARNING

Huxley

Reading and Writing
Third Edition
www.els.edu

Taken from:

Advanced Reading Power: Extensive Reading, Vocabulary Building, Comprehension Skills, Reading Faster
by Beatrice S. Mikulecky and Linda Jeffries

Writing Academic English: Level 4, The Longman Academic Writing Series, Fourth Edition
by Alice Oshima and Ann Hogue

Writing to Communicate 3: Essays and the Short Research Paper
by Cynthia A. Boardman

Academic Connections 4
by Julia Williams

Focus on Vocabulary 2: Mastering the Academic Word List, Second Edition
by Diane Schmitt and Norbert Schmitt

Eye on Editing 2: Developing Editing Skills for Writing
by Joyce S. Cain

A World of Fiction: Twenty Timeless Short Stories, Second Edition
by Sybil Marcus

American Perspectives: Readings on Contemporary U.S. Culture
by Susan Earle-Carlin and Colleen Hildebrand

More Reading Power 3: Reading for Pleasure, Comprehension Skills, Thinking Skills, Reading Faster, Second Edition
by Beatrice S. Mikulecky and Linda Jeffries

Cover images courtesy of traffic_analyzer/iStockphoto and Kuklev/iStockphoto.

Development Project Manager: Courtney Towson

Photo Editor: Jamie Wilson

Production Project Manager: Theresa Festa

Associate Aquisitions Editor: Pamela Vitu

Taken from:

*Advanced Reading Power:
Extensive Reading, Vocabulary
Building, Comprehension Skills,
Reading Faster*
by Beatrice S. Mikulecky and Linda
Jeffries
Copyright © 2007 by Pearson
Education, Inc.
Published by Pearson Longman
White Plains, New York 10606

*Writing Academic English: Level 4,
The Longman Academic Writing
Series,* Fourth Edition
by Alice Oshima and Ann Hogue
Copyright © 2006 by Pearson
Education, Inc.
Published by Pearson Longman

*Writing to Communicate 3: Essays
and the Short Research Paper*
by Cynthia A. Boardman
Copyright © 2009 by Pearson
Education, Inc.
Published by Pearson Longman

Academic Connections 4
by Julia Williams
Copyright © 2010 by Pearson
Education, Inc.
Published by Pearson Longman

*Focus on Vocabulary 2: Mastering
the Academic Word List,*
Second Edition
by Diane Schmitt and Norbert
Schmitt
Copyright © 2011 by Pearson
Education, Inc.
Published by Pearson Longman

*Eye on Editing 2: Developing
Editing Skills for Writing*
by Joyce S. Cain
Copyright © 2003 by Pearson
Education, Inc.
Published by Longman

*A World of Fiction: Twenty
Timeless Short Stories,* Second
Edition
by Sybil Marcus
Copyright © 2006 by Pearson
Education, Inc.
Published by Longman

*American Perspectives: Readings
on Contemporary U.S. Culture*
by Susan Earle-Carlin and Colleen
Hildebrand
Copyright © 2000 by Pearson
Education, Inc.
Published by Pearson Longman

*More Reading Power 3: Reading
for Pleasure, Comprehension
Skills, Thinking Skills, Reading
Faster,* Second Edition
by Beatrice S. Mikulecky and Linda
Jeffries
Copyright © 1996, 2002 by
Pearson Education, Inc.
Published by Pearson Longman

All trademarks, service marks, registered trademarks,
and registered service marks are the property of
their respective owners and are used herein for
identification purposes only.

Pearson Learning Solutions, 501 Boylston Street,
Suite 900,
Boston, MA 02116
A Pearson Education Company
www.pearsoned.com

Printed in the United States of America

1 2 3 4 5 6 7 8 9 10 VO31 17 16 15 14 13

000200010271295688

CT/JW

ISBN 10: 1-256-74220-1
ISBN 13: 978-1-256-74220-3

To the Teacher

Our focus in creating this textbook has been to create active rather than passive readers and writers through the practice of reading, analyzing, summarizing, sharing and reflecting in both oral and written forms.

In designing *Huxley* we used a variety of resources to provide learners with authentic readings of high interest to improve reading comprehension and speed, expand vocabulary, and build critical thinking skills. The topics were chosen to stimulate discussion and thought, and to act as a platform for written expression. The emphasis in this text is on **cause and effect**.

To the Student

The *Huxley* book begins with writing instruction for the **cause and effect** essay. The related reading and writing tasks are designed to provide comprehensive exposure, instruction, and practice in this style. A unit on fiction is also included. At the end of this text, there are appendices offering valuable supplementary material with vocabulary development, speed reading exercises, transition signal word charts, and additional grammar exercises for reference and further practice.

Contents

Contents

Scope & Sequence

Unit	Reading Skills	Writing Skills	Rhetorical Skills	Vocabulary
Intro		Identifying essay versus paragraph organization		Collocations
1	Identifying a thesis statement; analyzing a cause-effect essay	Organizing a cause-effect essay; using a hook; writing a cause-effect essay; editing	Cause-effect	Collocations
2	Highlighting; connecting graphics to writing	Note-taking; writing questions for more effective reading		Understanding vocabulary in context; word forms
3	Global reading; focused reading	Integrated writing		
4	Reading fiction; identifying style and point of view	Writing about literature		Verbs of movement; adjectives
5	Reading for vocabulary			Word families; collocations
Appendices	Increasing reading speed	Adjective clauses; connecting words and transition signals; punctuation rules; writing evaluations		Connecting words and transition signals

Acknowledgments

The Third Edition of our ELS SSP and Reading & Writing tests is the culmination of nearly two-and-a-half years of hard work by countless individuals from ELS Language Centers in the US, Canada, and Australia. This project began in the winter of 2011 when we convened our Curriculum Revision Committee. The fourteen teachers, Academic Directors and Center Directors who sat on this committee and saw the process through from start to finish are deserving of individual recognition for their tireless work: Lesley Carroll, Morgan Foster, Raylene Houck, Liz Hurysz, Dan Manolescu, Catherine Mason, Bernadette McGlynn, Mary McKay, Gerardo Mestizo, Scott Myers, Jim Scofield, Marie Silva, Carol Wright, and Lisagail Zeitlin.

This committee used their years of classroom teaching experience, study in curriculum design and ESL methodology, and intimate understanding of our ELS students to complete this tremendous task. The project involved, among other things, reviewing and refining specific language skills objectives for each level and text, reviewing hundreds of ESL texts, creating content, and organizing thematic units following a communicative approach to language instruction. Two sessions of piloting, five rounds of editing, and 27 months later, I am proud to present these texts to our ELS students.

I would also like to thank the 26 ELS centers and their academic teams that volunteered to pilot these texts, and over 50 ELS teachers who provided invaluable feedback. The feedback from teachers who used the texts gave us important insight into the practical use of these texts in the classroom and provided the basis for hundreds of edits and improvements.

A special thanks also to Terri Rapoport, Director of Curriculum Development, Susan Matson, Director of Teacher Training and Development, and Ward Morrow, Director of Academic Affairs, who, in addition to editing the texts, worked closely with our Curriculum Revision Committee and provided guidance, support, and advice.

In addition, we would like to thank Pearson Education, our publishing partner, for their collaborative effort in the preparation of the new edition. We'd also like to add a particular note of thanks to the Pearson Learning Solutions Rights Management group for their work in providing a significant amount of photo research for the series. The new photos help to shape the book and make it a more effective teaching and learning tool in print and digital formats.

Finally, thank you to all our academic staff and students for your belief in the power of teaching and learning English—and helping the world communicate better. May we all contribute to more peace, friendship, and understanding among all peoples of the world.

Mark W. Harris
President and CEO
ELS Educational Services

Introduction
The Process of Writing

The Arts. *Portrait of Dr. Gachet* by Vincent Van Gogh

WRITING FOCUS

Imagine that you have just entered your first class in a college or university, and you have just been given your first homework assignment, which is to write an essay that is due in two days. How do you handle this assignment?

If you are not sure, you may be surprised to discover that your classmates may be equally uncertain. Written language is different from spoken language, and essay writing is a particular form of written language with its own style and organization. In addition, different languages are organized differently in writing. Therefore, both native speakers and non-native speakers have to learn how to write in academic English.

It is important to learn the English academic style of writing because this is the type of organization that your professor will be expecting. The **paragraph** is the basic unit of organization. Once you know how to write an academic paragraph, you can easily expand that knowledge to write **essays** and **research papers**.

1. Paragraph Organization

Most of the paragraphs that you write will be for the body of an essay. These paragraphs typically have three parts: the **topic sentence**, **the body**, and the **concluding sentence**.

2. Essay Organization

In a university class, you will usually need to write more than a paragraph to present all of your information. Expanding a paragraph into an essay is easy now that you have a clear understanding of how to organize a paragraph. Like a paragraph, an essay has three parts:

- *the introductory paragraph*
- *body paragraphs*
- *the concluding paragraph*

Look at the diagram below. It shows how the model paragraph is expanded into an essay so that more information can be included.

Introduction   Above material from: *Writing to Communicate 3*

Now read the model essay, "The Traditional Music of the United States" and compare the organization to the chart you just looked at.

Model Essay

THE TRADITIONAL MUSIC OF THE UNITED STATES

What music truly belongs to one country? The traditional music of a country is becoming difficult to identify in this age of globalization. Still, there are rhythms, instruments, and melodies that seem to be uniquely Chinese or African or Jamaican. Even though it is a young country, the United States has also given birth to some unique musical styles. For example, jazz, country, and folk are three types of traditional music of the United States.

Jazz, the first type of traditional music in the United States, was born when the music of Africa blended with the music of Europe. Beginning in the seventeenth century, African people were brought to North America to be slaves. The Africans remembered their music, but the European slave owners didn't allow the Africans to play their own music. Therefore, the slaves incorporated European harmonies and melodies into the familiar music of their native land. However, jazz isn't the only music that developed from music brought from other lands.

The second type of traditional music, country, reflects the immigrant "melting pot" of the population of the United States. It developed from the Irish and English that settled in the Appalachian Mountains. As different immigrant populations arrived, sounds of different countries were added to the mix. Country music is characterized by steel guitars and powerful harmonies. The best-known type of country music comes from Nashville in Tennessee, where the Grand Ole Opry is located. Country music stars come to this concert hall and perform for enthusiastic audiences. The show is broadcast via radio. Because of this broadcast, the sound of country music has been spread to the rest of the United States and beyond.

Radio also helped spread the third type of traditional music. Folk music can be characterized by its acoustic guitars and its singers' voices. It gained national recognition in the 1930s and 1940s with such singers as Woody Guthrie and Pete Seeger. The height of its popularity occurred in the 1950s and 1960s, when many singers wrote and sang songs to protest against war, discrimination, and injustice. Performers like Bob Dylan and Joan Baez brought people together in their commitment to making the world a better place.

In conclusion, the traditional music of the United States is like the traditional music of any country because it developed from the experiences of its people. Jazz came from the enslavement of African people, country music came from the mixing of immigrants from many nations, and folk music came from the blending of an acoustic guitar and a human voice.

What about you? Is music important to you? Why or why not? Share your answer with a classmate.

Unit One
The Cause-Effect Essay

Language and communication.

A. WRITING FOCUS

1. Cause and Effect

A common approach to academic writing is to **analyze** a topic by taking it apart and examining each part. One way to do this is to look at the **causes** and **effects** of a situation. In other words, you analyze the reasons and examine the results. For example, you may analyze an event in history by discussing what led to the event and then describing what the result of the event was.

2. Determining True Cause and Effect Relationships

Read each situation below with a classmate. Determine the cause and the effect. Then decide whether the cause and effect relationship is valid.

1. If they have enough sunlight and water, most plants will grow.

2. Wayne must have learned Japanese because he spent three years living in Japan.

3. The French midterm exam was too hard. As a result, I failed it.

4. The mayor stole money from the city and left the country. Because of this, there is no money for language classes at the elementary school.

5. The Icelandic language hasn't changed much, so children there can read ancient texts.

6. I assume that Nadia speaks Russian since both of her parents do.

3. Identifying Causes and Effects

*Work with a classmate. For each topic, write **C** if the item below is a cause, **E** if it is an effect, **CE** if it is both, and **X** if it is neither. Discuss your choices.*

1. miscommunication

   _____ speaking a different language   _____ losing a job

   _____ not hearing   _____ sending an e-mail

   _____ not paying attention   _____ feeling embarrassed

2. fast communication

   _____ carrying cell phones   _____ using e-mail

   _____ being connected all the time   _____ feeling pressured

   _____ hating being alone   _____ text-messaging

3. learning another language

   _____ reading books   _____ finding a job

   _____ communicating with foreigners   _____ falling in love

   _____ conducting business   _____ traveling

4. Writing an Essay Outline

Good essay writers study the characteristics of organization to learn how to write, but they also learn by reading other essays. In other essays, they can see not only the basics of essay writing but also the many variations on those basics. Then they can pattern their own writing on what they have read.

   Outlining is a good way to understand the organization of a piece of writing as well as a good way to organize your own writing. When you outline an essay while reading it, you learn how to outline and organize your own essays. Your outlines can be very simple, with just one or two words for each paragraph, or they can be more detailed with information about topic sentences and supporting sentences.

Most cause and effect essays follow one of two basic organizational patterns. The first discusses all the causes and/or effects separately in "blocks." A block can be one or more paragraphs. The block style has two common variations. In one you discuss both causes and effects, and in the other you discuss only causes or only effects. In the second basic pattern, you have a series of one-cause/one-effect paragraphs, where each cause is "linked" to one effect. The simple outlines below show these patterns.

Block Pattern 1	**Block Pattern 2**	**Linking Pattern**
I. Introduction	I. Introduction	I. Introduction
II. Causes	II. Cause *or* Effect	II. Cause → Effect
III. Effects	III. Cause *or* Effect	III. Cause → Effect
IV. Conclusion	IV. Cause *or* Effect	IV. Cause → Effect
	V. Conclusion	V. Conclusion

5. Outlining an Essay

As you read Model Essay 1, complete the outline which follows. Which pattern does this essay represent?

Model Essay 1

CHANGES IN THE ENGLISH LANGUAGE

That English, like all languages, has changed over the years is clear to any student of English literature who tries to read Chaucer[1]. The English that he wrote in the twelfth century is nearly unintelligible today. Unfortunately, this is the first effect of language change: a barrier[2] to understanding. *Why* languages change is another topic—one that can be analyzed. In general, linguists agree that there are two basic causes of language change: simplification and contact with other languages.

Over time, speakers simplify a language by making it more efficient. The pronunciation of English, for example, has undergone change in order to make it easier. For example, researchers have determined that words in Old English were spoken almost exactly as they were written. Because of this, we know that in Old English, the "gh" in *bought* was pronounced. However, pronouncing the *gh* before the *t* is not an efficient use of the mouth, so in Modern English, the *gh* is silent. Anyone who has tried to figure out the spelling system of English knows that there are many words with silent letters: *debt, know, honor, autumn, business, whole, build.*

Another way of simplifying a language also leads to change. Speakers often make analogies between grammatical structures within the language in order to regularize them. For example, many irregular verbs in English have changed due to the desire to simplify. The changes are made by making an analogy between regular verbs and irregular verbs. The past tense of such irregular verbs as *burn* and *dream* used to be *burnt*

[1]**Chaucer** *proper n.* Geoffrey Chaucer (?1340–1400), an English writer known for his long poem *The Canterbury Tales*, one of the most important works in English literature
[2]**barrier** *n.* something that prevents people from doing something

and *dreamt*, but they have regularized to *burned* and *dreamed*. In short, one major cause of language change is the desire of speakers to simplify it.

The second major cause of language change happens when speakers of different languages come in contact. This is particularly true with vocabulary. Everyone can recognize common cognates[3], such as *hospital* from the French *hôpital*. However, few speakers of English know that such everyday words as *banana, chocolate, hey, ketchup,* and *magazine* come from such diverse languages as Wolof (West Africa), Nahuatl (Central Mexico), Norwegian, Chinese, and Arabic, respectively. In fact, nearly one third of all English words can trace their origin back to French. This is because, in 1066, the Normans of present-day France conquered England and became the ruling class for 300 years. There are even leftover structures of French grammar in English.

For example, in English, adjectives come before nouns, but in French, adjectives come after nouns. There are set phrases in English, however, that still have the adjective after the noun: *president elect, surgeon general, times past,* and *stage left*. These phrases don't change; that is, the combination of noun and adjective isn't separated. However, there are a few adjectives, such as *proper* and *aplenty*, which are used more freely. For example, speakers can say that they live in *New York proper* or *San Francisco proper*, and that they have *apples aplenty* or *friends aplenty*.

In short, English, like other languages, is always changing. Speakers attempt to simplify the pronunciation and grammar to make them more efficient. When English speakers come in contact with speakers of languages, both languages will influence each other by adopting vocabulary and even some grammatical structures. For linguists, these changes are the heart of their research, but for an everyday speaker of a language, the changes can also be of interest. You are living during a time of changes in your language. Can you spot any?

What about you? Can you think of any words in your language that have been borrowed from English? Share your answer with a classmate.

  I. Introductory paragraph
     A. Hook

        1. _____
        2. Transition to causes of language change
     B. Thesis statement
        1. Two basic causes of language change

           a. _____
           b. Contact with other languages

  II. Simplify by making language more efficient

     A. _____

        1. _____

        2. _____

---

[3]**cognate** *n.* a word that has a similar meaning and spelling in two languages, such as *address* (English) and *Adresse* (German)

    B. Bridge to next paragraph

      1. Analogies between grammatical structure to regularize

        a. _____

        b. _____

    C. Concluding sentence

III. _____

    A. _____

      1. Examples: banana, chocolate, hey, ketchup, magazine

      2. _____

    B. Bridge to next paragraph

    C. Some N ADJ in English

      1. Static phrases that don't change

      2. _____

IV. Concluding paragraph

    A. Restatement of thesis

    B. Final comment

6. Reorganizing an Essay

Complete the outline of Model Essay 2, which is organized according to Block Pattern 2. Then, using the same information, complete the Linking Pattern outline.

Model Essay 2

NONVERBAL MISCOMMUNICATION

Misunderstandings between people happen for many reasons. This can be especially true when two people have different language and cultural backgrounds. It's clear how people who don't speak the same language can be misunderstood, but understanding what people are saying when they aren't speaking can be equally problematic. Cultural differences in nonverbal communication can cause considerable cultural misunderstandings.

Nonverbal signals are learned at a very young age by observing the people in your culture. Eye contact is very culturally dependent. In some cultures, making eye contact is essential to communication, while in other cultures, it is a sign of disrespect. The distance that people stand apart from each other is also culturally determined. In addition, what you do with your hands and how you gesture with them are culturally bound forms of communication. The effects of these cultural differences do not cause misunderstandings with people with similar cultural backgrounds, but they can lead to comical as well as serious misunderstanding between people raised in different cultures.

For example, in North American cultures, it is usual for people to look each other in the eye when they are talking. If one person doesn't, the other person may think that the first person is lying or being evasive[1]. However, in many Asian cultures, it is considered

___

[1]**evasive** *adj.* not willing to answer questions directly

impolite to look someone in the eye, especially in the workplace with people in a higher position. This simple difference can lead to direct misunderstanding between people from these countries. The North Americans will probably think that the Asians are hiding something, and the Asians will probably think that the North Americans are being rude.

In the United States, it is common for people of European descent[2] to stand about eighteen inches, or the length of an arm, apart when they are having a conversation. On the other hand, people of Central and South American heritage stand much closer to each other—about a foot closer. This difference can cause a "dance" in which the European American keeps backing up to maintain an eighteen-inch separation, while the Latino keeps stepping closer to narrow the gap. The result is that the Latino may think that the European American is trying to avoid him or her. On the other hand, the European American may think that the Latino is sending a romantic message since being closer than a foot is a sign of intimacy[3] in the European American's mind.

A difference in meaning with one gesture can cause a somewhat comical misunderstanding. In the United States, people wave goodbye to each other by lifting their arm and, with the palm of the hand facing out, moving the hand up and down or back and forth. However, a very similar gesture means "come here" in many Asian countries. Therefore, just as the Asian is asking the North American to come closer to him or her, the North American is waving goodbye and going in the opposite direction.

In conclusion, when you are interacting with people of different cultures, it's a good idea to learn how they communicate—both verbally and nonverbally. Not understanding the customs of eye contact, personal space, and gestures can cause a lot of miscommunication—both comical and serious.

Block Pattern 2	**Linking Pattern**
I. Introduction	I. Introduction
II. Cultural differences	II. _____
A. _____	A. North American
B. _____	B. Asian
C. Gestures	III. Cultural differences lead to misunderstandings due to differences in personal space
III. Effects of differences in eye contact	A. _____
IV. _____	B. _____
V. _____	IV. _____
VI. Conclusion	A. _____
	B. _____
	V. Conclusion

[2]**descent** *n.* your family origins, especially in relation to the country where your family came from
[3]**intimacy** *n.* a state of having a close, personal relationship with someone

7. Introductory Paragraphs

An essay begins with an introductory paragraph, which ends with the thesis statement. What comes before the thesis statement must "hook" the reader; that is, it must make the reader want to read your essay. In addition, the transition from the hook to the thesis statement must be clear. Sometimes the transition is just a word, and sometimes it is a sentence. There are several ways to hook the reader.

Cause and Effect Hooks

In an essay that discusses the causes only, a good introductory paragraph may briefly mention the **effects**. Similarly, in an essay only about the effects of something, your introductory paragraph could briefly mention the **causes**. In this introductory paragraph from Model Essay 1, the mention of an effect of language change leads to the thesis statement about the causes of language change.

Model Introductory Paragraph 1

Effects of Languages Changing	That English, like all languages, has changed over the years is clear to any student of English literature who tries to read Chaucer. The English that he wrote in the twelfth century is nearly unintelligible today. Unfortunately, this is the first effect of language change: a barrier to understanding.
Connecting Sentence	Why languages change is another topic—one that can be analyzed.
Thesis Statement	In general, linguists agree that there are two basic causes of language change: simplification for efficiency or regularity and contact with other languages.

General-to-Specific Hooks

A common hook begins with a **general point** and narrows it down to a **specific point**, which is your thesis statement. In this introductory paragraph from Model Essay 2, the topic of "misunderstandings" starts very broad and narrows to the thesis statement.

Model Introductory Paragraph 2

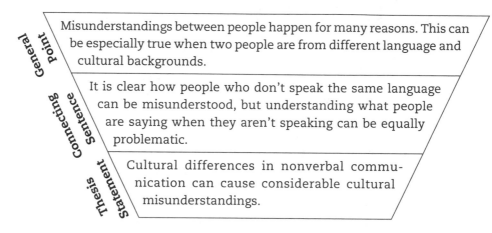

Misunderstandings between people happen for many reasons. This can be especially true when two people are from different language and cultural backgrounds.

It is clear how people who don't speak the same language can be misunderstood, but understanding what people are saying when they aren't speaking can be equally problematic.

Cultural differences in nonverbal communication can cause considerable cultural misunderstandings.

Personal Anecdote Hooks

Another way of introducing your thesis statement is to write a **personal anecdote**, or story, about an event that is relevant to the topic. Model 3 is this type of hook.

Model Introductory Paragraph 3

Personal Anecdote	I have lived in the United States for over 20 years now. I moved here in my early twenties, alone and without my family, in order to attend college. As so often happens, I met a man, fell in love, and married him. I travel home as often as possible, but the time between visits is getting longer and longer. Even though I can still speak my native language, I find it increasingly difficult to remember words. In fact, I find it easier to use English, and my relatives back home are happy to use English with me since they want to practice. As the years go by, I feel more at ease in English.
Connecting Sentence	This upsets and surprises me.
Thesis Statement	People can lose comfort in their own native languages in several different ways.

Historical Hooks

Another type of hook gives a **historical perspective** on your topic. In this type of hook, you write about an event in history that relates to your topic. Model 4 discusses the historical context in which the English language changed, which is the topic of Model Essay 1.

Model Introductory Paragraph 4

Historical Background	In 1066, the Duke of Normandy, also known as William the Conqueror, succeeded in defeating the English armies, which marked the beginning of profound changes in English rule. England became less influenced by Scandinavia and closer to the countries of the European continent.
Connecting Sentence	This influence penetrated all parts of life, including culture and commerce.
Thesis Statement	The English language as well underwent many changes during this period.

8. Writing Introductory Paragraphs

Choose a cause and effect topic and write a thesis statement. Then write two different types of introductory paragraphs for the thesis statement.

B. SENTENCE FOCUS

1. Avoiding Stringy Sentences

If you combine too many independent clauses, you may end up with a **stringy sentence**. A stringy sentence has too many independent clauses, perhaps through an overuse of coordinating conjunctions or subordinating conjunctions. For example:

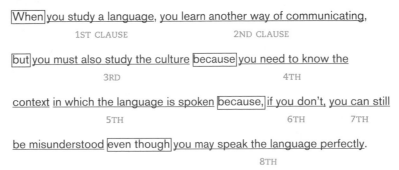

When you study a language, you learn another way of communicating,
      1ST CLAUSE   2ND CLAUSE

but you must also study the culture because you need to know the
      3RD   4TH

context in which the language is spoken because, if you don't, you can still
      5TH   6TH   7TH

be misunderstood even though you may speak the language perfectly.
      8TH

One way to make this sentence less stringy is to divide it into two sentences by using a transition instead of a coordinating conjunction. Here is a list of the transitions that mean the same as the coordinating conjunctions:

Coordinating Conjunction	Transition
and	moreover in addition
but yet	however on the other hand
so	therefore as a result

Here is the stringy sentence divided into two sentences by using a transition instead of the coordinating conjunction:

When you study a language, you learn another way of communicating.
　　1ST CLAUSE　　　　　　　　　　　2ND

However, you must also study the culture because you need to know the
　　　　　　1ST CLAUSE　　　　　　　　　　　　2ND

context in which the language is spoken because, if you don't, you can still
　　　　　3RD　　　　　　　　　　　　　　4TH　　　　　5TH

be misunderstood even though you may speak the language perfectly.
　　　　　　　　　　　　　　6TH

This is now less stringy, but it still needs work. The second sentence has six clauses—one independent clause, one adjective clause, and four adverbial clauses. By changing an adverbial clause into a separate sentence, you can make the sentence even less stringy. Below is a list of subordinating conjunctions and the transitions that have similar meanings:

Subordinating Conjunction	Transition
after	after that next
before	before that previously
while	meanwhile
even though although	nevertheless nonetheless
whereas while	on the other hand in contrast
if	otherwise

Here is the stringy sentence now divided into three sentences. Since it is no longer stringy, it is easier to understand.

When you study a language, you learn another way of communicating.
     1ST CLAUSE   2ND

However, you must also study the culture because you need to know the
     1ST CLAUSE   2ND

context in which the language is spoken. **Otherwise,** you can still be
     3RD   1ST CLAUSE

misunderstood even though you may speak the language perfectly.
                2ND

2. Rewriting Stringy Sentences

Work with a classmate and rewrite each of the following sentences to make them less stringy.

1. When I moved to a small village in Croatia, I didn't speak the language, so it was hard for me to talk with people because most Croatians at that time didn't speak English, but I found a tutor, and I learned Croatian, so by the time I left Croatia ten months later, I spoke the language fairly well.

2. Snapping your fingers to get someone's attention is a common gesture in many countries, but in the United States it is considered a very rude way to get someone's attention, so this gesture should be avoided when you travel to the United States.

3. Since English has many French and German words, there are many false cognates, so French and German speaking learners of English have to be careful when they use English because they may be misunderstood.

4. Blanche's mother is French, and her father is Turkish, so she learned both languages when she was growing up although she mostly speaks English now because she is married to a Canadian.

5. When I was visiting Kiri today, her mother, who doesn't speak English, wanted me to see a painting in her room, so she gestured to me to follow her, but I misunderstood and thought that she wanted me to leave, so I started waving goodbye while she kept gesturing to me to follow her.

C. Language Focus

1. Collocations

Collocations are two or more words that commonly go together. Collocations are common in academic writing, and using them correctly can add to the sophistication of your writing. Study the sentences below that use common collocations for cause and effect.

Phrasal Verb Collocations

- *The Norman invasion **brought about** a change in English vocabulary.*
- *Contact with other languages **brings forth** changes in vocabulary.*
- *The desire for easy pronunciation in the past **gave rise to** very difficult spelling nowadays.*
- *Speaking a new language **leads to** better fluency.*
- *Spelling changes often **result from** a desire for greater simplicity.*

Adjective and Noun Collocations

- The **immediate cause** of the death of the Yana language was the death of its last native speaker.
- The **underlying cause** was the near total destruction of the Yana people by the European settlers in California.
- A **likely cause** of frustration when speaking your native language is not remembering words.
- An **unlikely cause** is that you're forgetting your native language.
- Spending a year in Chile had the **desired effect.** I learned Spanish.
- We may never know the **full effect** of losing so many languages.
- The speaker's accent had a **modest effect** on the audience's understanding of his lecture.

Idiom Collocations

- Students often **feel the effects of** learning a second language most at the end of the day when their brains can't think in any language!
- You may **suffer the consequences of** not studying your vocabulary.
- Our lack of understanding of common nonverbal gestures **set the foundation for** our total frustration.

2. Using Collocations

Fill in each blank with one of the collocations given in the box above the paragraph. There are two extra collocations in each box. You can use each collocation only once.

resulted from	gave rise to
the desired effect	the immediate cause
feel the effects of	a modest effect

1. Hawaiian Pidgin, spoken in the Hawaiian islands, first _____ language contact among English settlers and the native Hawaiian people. Then, in the 1800s, immigrants from China, Japan, Korea, Portugal, and the Philippines came to Hawaii to work on the sugar plantations. Obviously, the workers needed to communicate with each other and the English and Hawaiian-speaking plantation owners, and this need _____ another form of Pidgin. The new language had _____; workers and owners were able to communicate. Linguistically, the other languages had _____ on English grammar; the grammar of Pidgin is actually quite close to that of English. They had a larger effect on vocabulary, with such words as *pau* for *finished*, from Hawaiian, and *akamai* for *smart*, from Japanese. Some expressions are reductions of English words, such as *brah* (brother) and *howzit?* (How's it going?). When you visit

Hawaii, keep your ears open for Pidgin and see if you can understand it. Then try to learn some yourself!

a modest effect	set the foundation for
bring forth	the full effect of
led to	the underlying cause of

2. _____ the renaissance of the Welsh language is the fact the Welsh

people didn't want their language to die out. This desire _____

many parents speaking Welsh to their children at home. The determination of the

Welsh people also _____ Welsh schools, a new Welsh publish-

ing industry, and a lot more people speaking Welsh in the streets of such Welsh

cities as Cardiff and Bangor. No doubt, _____ the rebirth of this

beloved language is still to come.

D. WRITING TO COMMUNICATE

1. Your Turn

Choose one of the topics below, and write a cause and/or effect essay. Follow the steps of the writing process (analyzing the topic, brainstorming, organizing, writing the first draft, rewriting, writing the final draft).

1. Review the three aspects of nonverbal communication that were discussed in Model Essay 1 in terms of your culture. Then give some personal examples of the effects of misunderstandings based on those aspects.

2. What are the effects of our use of written communication, such as e-mail, instant messaging, or phone text messaging, on communication?

3. Why did you decide to learn another language? How has your life changed because of it?

2. Peer Help Worksheet

Trade essays and textbooks with a classmate. Read your classmate's essay while your classmate reads yours. Check off (✓) the items in your partner's book as you evaluate them. Then return the essays and books. If any of the items in your book are not checked off, and you agree with your partner, correct your essay before turning it in. Use a pencil if you write on your classmate's essay or book. Refer to the chart on page 18.

Content

1. Is the topic appropriate for a cause and effect essay? ☐

2. Are the causes and effects clearly explained? ☐

Organization

1. Does the introductory paragraph grab the reader's attention? ☐

   What does the hook do? (Check one.)

   a. Discusses causes or effects ☐

   b. Starts with general information and leads to the specific thesis statement ☐

   c. Gives a personal anecdote ☐

   d. Gives a historical perspective ☐

2. Circle the thesis statement. Underline the controlling idea.

3. Are the body paragraphs well organized? ☐

   a. Do they have topic sentences? ☐

   b. Do they have concluding sentences? ☐

   c. Do they use transitions? ☐

4. What elements of concluding paragraphs does the concluding paragraph in this essay have? (Check all that apply.)

   a. summary ☐

   b. restatement of the thesis statement ☐

   c. final comment ☐

Language

1. Has the writer avoided using stringy sentences? ☐

2. Are commas and semicolons used correctly? ☐

   If not, discuss any possible mistakes with the writer.

---

3. Writing to Communicate . . . More

As a journal entry or an in-class timed essay, choose one of the topics below. You can choose to focus on writing fluently, or you can practice any of the organizational techniques, sentence patterns, or language points discussed in this unit.

1. Analyze the causes and/or effects on language since the beginning of the electronic age.

2. Discuss some of the nonverbal miscommunications you have had with people from other cultures. Analyze the causes and effects of each.

3. How has globalization affected language?

Unit Two

Reading to Study

In this unit you will practice three strategies for studying texts so you can make sure that you learn and remember what you have read.

A. STRATEGY 1: TEXT MARKING

When you are reading a text that contains many facts and ideas, it is helpful to mark the important facts and ideas so that they stand out and can be used for reviewing and remembering the material.

1. What to Mark in a Text

You should select and make visually memorable only the most important information or ideas:

- *the topic of the passage*
- *the thesis statement, if the thesis is directly stated*
- *signals for the overall pattern of the passage*
- *the main idea*
- *the details that support the thesis or main idea, including key dates or names*
- *ideas that seem to differ from what you already know or have read about*
- *terms or points that are difficult to understand*

2. How to Mark a Text

The following is a list of different kinds of marking that good students often use. You should try out all of these techniques and then decide which ones work best for you. Experienced readers develop their own personal style of marking, usually a combination of various techniques.

- *Underlining (in pencil)*
- *Circling or making a box around words or phrases*
- *Drawing lines or arrows from one part of the text to another*
- *Writing a key word, date, or name in the margin*
- *Making a star or arrow in the margin beside an important point*
- *Making a question mark or exclamation point to express your reaction*
- *Numbering points in a series*

Note: Always preview a text before you read it and mark it. And always mark in pencil so you can make changes if necessary.

Example:

a. *Preview the passage below and then read it carefully. Look at the way it has been marked to identify the thesis, the pattern signals, and the supporting points.*

The Cultivation of the Pineapple

The pineapple has been cultivated and enjoyed by humans for thousands of years. According to archaeologists, evidence from drawings on ancient Peruvian pottery shows that Native Americans were cultivating the pineapple in about 1,000 A.D. Furthermore, some botanists believe that people in South and Central America began cultivating it *DEFINITION* much earlier. Cultivated pineapples do not produce seeds. This fact indicates that the plant has been dependent on humans for its reproduction for such a long time that it no longer can reproduce by itself.

When Europeans discovered the pineapple at the end of the fifteenth century, it was a case of love at first sight. Many of the early explorers reported favorably about this new fruit, saying that it had a delightful smell and a sweet, refreshing taste. In fact, of all the new American fruits that were brought back to Europe, the pineapple was the most successful. While other fruits, such as the tomato, were regarded with great suspicion and believed to be poisonous, the pineapple was accepted relatively quickly.

Throughout the sixteenth century, the ships of the European explorers carried pineapples from Central and South America to other parts of the world. During these voyages, the fruit provided an excellent source of fresh food and vitamins for the ship's crew. Furthermore, when they arrived the travelers found that, if the climate was suitable, it was easy to grow more fruit from the cut-off tops of pineapples. By the end of the sixteenth century, pineapples were being cultivated in parts of India, Africa, and China. In Europe, the climate was generally too cold, so the fruit could be grown only by wealthy people with heated greenhouses.

Pineapples remained a luxury food until the early twentieth century, when they became more easily available. Faster shipping and improved rail and road connections made it possible to bring the pineapples to new markets. Then, with the advent[1] of safe industrial canning methods, factories could produce canned pineapple for mass markets. As the fruit became more available and better known, demand rose rapidly for both fresh and canned pineapple. Production quickly expanded to meet that demand, most notably in Hawaii, which dominates the world market. Today, Puerto Rico, the Philippines, Kenya, and Thailand are also important pineapple producers.

b. *Use the text marking in the passage to help you write the following information.*

Overall pattern of organization: _____

Thesis statement: _____

_____

Supporting points (main ideas):

Paragraph 2: _____

[1]**advent:** beginning

Paragraph 3: _____

Paragraph 4: _____

c. *Compare your work with that of another student. If you disagree, look back at the text and explain your answers.*

d. *Preview the passage below and then read it carefully. Mark the text to show the thesis, the pattern signals, and supporting points. Try to use as many different kinds of markings as you can: underlining, marginal notes, circles, numbers, or arrows.*

THE HISTORY OF PIZZA

One of the most popular foods around the world today is pizza. Pizza restaurants are popular everywhere from Beijing to Moscow to Rio, and, even in the United States, the home of the hamburger, there are more pizza restaurants than hamburger places. This worldwide love for pizza is a fairly recent phenomenon. Before the 1950s, pizza was a purely Italian food, with a long history in southern Italy.

The origins of pizza are somewhat uncertain, though they may go back to the Greeks (*pita* bread) or even earlier. Under the Roman Empire, Italians often ate flat circles of bread, which they may have flavored with olive oil, cheese, and herbs. By about the year 1000 A.D. in the area around Naples, this bread had a name: *picea*.

This early kind of pizza lacked one of the main ingredients we associate with pizza: the tomato. In fact, tomatoes did not exist in Europe until the sixteenth century, when Spanish explorers brought them back from South America. The Spanish showed little interest in tomatoes, but southern Italians soon began to cultivate them and use them in cooking. At some point in the 1600s, Neapolitan tomatoes were added to *pizza*, as it was known by then.

The next development in pizza making came about, according to legend, in June 1889, when a Neapolitan pizza maker was asked to make pizza for the king and queen. To show his patriotism, he decided to make it green, white, and red, like the Italian flag, using basil leaves, mozzarella, and tomato. He named his pizza "Margherita," after the queen, and that is what this classic kind of pizza is still called today.

In Italy, pizza remained a specialty of Naples and other areas of the south until well into the twentieth century. Then, in the 1950s and 60s, when many southerners moved to the north to work in the new factories, pizzerias opened up in many northern Italian cities. By the 1980s, they could be found all over the country and pizza had become a part of the Italian way of life.

Today, pizza has become so common in so many countries that its Italian origins are often forgotten. Indeed, the global versions of pizza made with all kinds of ingredients have little in common with the Neapolitan original, as anyone knows who has tasted a pizza in Naples.

e. *Use your text marking in the passage to help you write the following information. Change your marking if it does not indicate these points.*

Overall pattern of organization: _____

Thesis statement: _____

_____

Supporting points (main ideas):

Paragraph 2: _____

Paragraph 3: _____

Paragraph 4: _____

Paragraph 5: _____

Paragraph 6: _____

f.   Compare your work with that of another student. If you disagree, look back at the text and explain your answers.

B. STRATEGY 2: WRITING QUESTIONS FOR MORE EFFECTIVE READING

1. In addition to marking a text, write study questions and quiz questions:

*   *Before you read, use the title, headings and subheadings to form questions about the text. This will help you focus your thinking.*
*   *When you have finished reading and marking the text, write quiz questions about the important facts and ideas to help reinforce your learning.*

Example:

a. Read this study question based on the title of the passage below, which is the introduction to a section of a sociology textbook.

Study question: *How is this passage going to analyze urbanization?*

b. Read the passage and look for the answer to the study question. Note facts and ideas that have been marked in the text.

A GLOBAL ANALYSIS OF URBANIZATION[1]

In 1693, William Penn wrote that "the country life is to be preferred for there we see the works of God, but in cities little else than the work of man." Most people at the time probably agreed with him. Less than 2 percent of the world's population then were urban dwellers.[2] But in 1998, about 44 percent of the world's population lived in urban areas and more than 50 percent will do so by the end of 2010 (Haub, 1999; Linden, 1993; Fischer, 1984).

While urban populations have grown, cities themselves have changed. We can identify three periods in their history: the preindustrial, industrial, and metropolitan-megalopolitan stages.   ①   ②   ③

[1]**urbanization:** development of cities
[2]**dweller:** resident

c. *Working with another student, answer the quiz questions below without looking back at the passage. Then check your answers by reading the passage again.*

1. <u>What percent of the world's population lived in cities in the 1600s?</u>

2. <u>How many lived in cities by the end of 2010?</u>

3. <u>What are the three different stages of urbanization that occurred over the years?</u>

2. a. *Preview the next section from the sociology textbook and write a study question from the title.*

Study question: _____

b. *Now read the section and mark the key facts and ideas in the text.*

THE PREINDUSTRIAL CITY

For more than 99 percent of the time that we humans have been on Earth, our ancestors have roamed about in search of food. They have hunted, fished, and gathered edible plants, but they have never found enough food in more than one place to sustain them for very long. They have had to move on, traveling in small bands from one place to another.

Then, about 10,000 years ago, technological advances allowed people to stop their wandering. This was the dawn of what is called the *Neolithic period*. People now had the simple tools and the know-how to cultivate plants and domesticate animals. They could produce their food supplies in one locale, and they settled down and built villages. The villages were very small—with only about 200 to 400 residents each. For the next 5,000 years, villagers produced just enough food to feed themselves.

About 5,000 years ago, humans developed more powerful technologies. Thanks to innovations like the ox-drawn plow, irrigation, and metallurgy, farmers could produce more food than they needed to sustain themselves and their families. Because of this food surplus, some people abandoned agriculture and made their living by weaving, making pottery, and practicing other specialized crafts. Methods of transporting and storing food were also improved. The result was the emergence of cities.

Cities first arose on the fertile banks of such rivers as the Nile of Egypt, the Euphrates and Tigris in the Middle East, the Indus in Pakistan, and the Yellow River in China. Similar urban settlements later appeared in other parts of the world. The *preindustrial* cities were small compared with the cities of today. Most had populations of 5,000 to 10,000 people. Only a few cities had more than 100,000 and even Rome never had more than several hundred thousand.

Several factors prevented expansion of the preindustrial city. By modern standards, agricultural techniques were still primitive. It took at least 75 farmers to produce enough of a surplus to support just one city dweller. For transportation, people had to depend on their own muscle power or that of animals. It was difficult to carry food supplies from farms to cities, and even more difficult to transport heavy materials for construction in the cities. Poor sanitation, lack of sewer facilities, and ineffective medicine kept the death rate high. Epidemics regularly killed as much as half of a city's population. Moreover, families still had a strong attachment to the land, which discouraged immigration to the cities. All these characteristics of preindustrial society kept the cities small (Davis, 1955).

Reprinted from *Sociology: A Brief Introduction*, Sixth Edition (2005), Allyn & Bacon, a Pearson Education Company.

c. Compare your study question and text markings with those of another student. If you disagree, look back at the text to explain your work. Then write three quiz questions about this section.

1. _____

2. _____

3. _____

d. Ask another pair of students to answer your questions without looking back at the text. Then check the text for the answers.

3. *a.* Preview the next section from the sociology textbook and write a study question from the title.

Study question: _____

b. Now read the section and mark the key facts and ideas in the text.

THE INDUSTRIAL CITY

For almost 5,000 years, cities changed little. Then their growth, in size and number, was so rapid that it has been called an *urban revolution* or *urban explosion*. In 1700, less than 2 percent of the population of Great Britain lived in cities, but by 1900, the majority of the British did so. Other European countries and the United States soon achieved the same level of urbanization in an even shorter period. Today, these and other Western countries are among the most urbanized in the world, along with many Latin American countries, which have become mostly urbanized in more recent years.

The major stimulus to the urban explosion was the Industrial Revolution. It triggered a series of related events, identified by sociologist Philip Hauser (1981) as population explosion, followed by population displosion and population implosion, and then by technoplosion. Industrialization first causes a rise in production growth, and the mechanization of farming brings about an agricultural surplus. Fewer farmers can support more people—and thus larger urban populations (*population explosion*). Workers no longer needed on the farms move to the city. There is, then, displacement of people from rural to urban areas (*population displosion*) and a greater concentration of people in a limited area (*population implosion*). The development of other new technologies (*technoplosion*) spurs on urbanization. Improved transportation, for example, speeds the movement of food and other materials to urban centers.

The outcome of these events was the *industrial city*. Compared with the preindustrial city, the industrial city was larger, more densely settled, and more diverse. It was a place where large numbers of people—with a wide range of skills, interests, and cultural backgrounds—could live and work together in a limited space. Also, unlike the preindustrial city, which had served primarily as a religious or governmental center, the industrial city was a commercial hub. In fact, its abundant job opportunities attracted so many rural migrants that migration accounted for the largest share of its population growth. Without these migrants, cities would not have grown at all because of the high mortality rate brought about by extremely poor sanitary conditions.

c. *Compare your study question and text markings with those of another student. If you disagree, look back at the text to explain your work. Then write three quiz questions about this section.*

1. _____

2. _____

3. _____

d. *Ask another pair of students to answer your questions without looking back at the text. Then check the text for the answers.*

4. a. *Preview the next section from the sociology textbook and write a study question from the title.*

Study question: _____

b. *Now read the section and mark the key facts and ideas in the text.*

METROPOLIS AND MEGALOPOLIS

Early in this century, the large cities of the industrialized nations began to spread outward. They formed **metropolises**, large urban areas that include a city and its surrounding suburbs. Some of these suburbs are politically separate from their central cities, but socially, economically, and geographically, the suburbs and the city are tied together. The U.S. Census Bureau recognizes this unity by defining what is called a *Standard Metropolitan Statistical Area*, which cuts across political boundaries. Since 1990, most U.S. residents have been living in metropolitan areas with 1 million residents or more (Suro, 1991).

In the United States, the upper and middle classes have usually sparked[1] the expansion of cities outward. Typically, as migrants from rural areas moved into the central city, the wealthier classes moved to the suburbs. The automobile greatly facilitated this development. It encouraged people to leave the crowded inner city for the more comfortable life of the suburbs, if they could afford it. As the number of cars increased, so did the size of suburbs and metropolises. In 1900, there were only 8,000 cars in the United States; by 1930, the number had soared to more than 26 million. Meanwhile, the proportion of the U.S. population living in the suburbs grew from only 15.7 percent in 1910 to 49.6 percent in 1950 (Glaab and Brown, 1983).

Since 1950, virtually all the growth in metropolitan areas has occurred in the suburbs. During the 1960s, U.S. suburbs grew four times faster than inner cities, and stores and entertainment facilities followed the people there. Suburban jobs increased 44 percent, while inner-city employment dropped 7 percent. This pattern of suburban growth at the expense of the urban core continued in the 1970s and 1980s. Today, suburbanites outnumber city residents three to two (U.S. Census Bureau, 2003; Gottdiener, 1983; Jaaret, 1983).

As suburbs expand, they sometimes combine with the suburbs of adjacent metropolitan areas to form a **megalopolis**, a vast area in which many metropolises merge.[2] For hundreds of miles from one major city to the next, suburbs and cities have merged with one another to form a continuous region in which distinctions between suburban, urban, and rural areas are blurred.[3] The hundreds of miles from Boston to Washington, D.C., form

[1]**spark:** to cause
[2]**merge:** to join together
[3]**blurred:** not clear

one such megalopolis; another stretches from Detroit through Chicago to Milwaukee in the Midwest; and a third goes from San Francisco to San Diego.

    c. Compare your study question and text markings with those of another student. If you disagree, look back at the text to explain your work. Then write three quiz questions about this section.

        1. _____

        2. _____

        3. _____

    d. Ask another pair of students to answer your questions without looking back at the text. Then check the text for the answers.

5. *a. Preview the next section from the sociology textbook and write a study question from the title.*

    Study question: _____

    b. Now read the section and mark the key facts and ideas in the text.

THE WORLD'S MEGACITIES

The world's urban population has grown so fast that today, there are about 40 megacities—cities with populations of 5 million or more. Generally, the poorer the country, the faster its urban growth. Thus, today, only three of the world's megacities are in the United States, and more than half are in developing countries. Many more cities in the developing world will soon become megacities.

Since the emergence of the pre-industrial city 5,000 years ago, great cities have risen and fallen. The same is true today. One city that is collapsing[1] is Kinshasa, the capital of Zaire. Although the country is endowed with[2] abundant natural resources, such as gold, diamonds, copper, and rich agricultural land, Kinshasa has produced massive miseries under the corrupt[3] 30-year-reign of former President Sese Mobutu. Government officials have routinely looted[4] manufactured goods, fuel, food, and medical supplies, even most of the emergency food aid sent by foreign countries. As a result, the annual inflation rate[5] has often soared to more than 3,000 percent and the jobless rate to 80 percent, posing serious threats of starvation and epidemics. In contrast, the city of Curitiba in Brazil is a success story. The city is not rich, but its government makes the most of its resources. One example is recycling: Parks are lit with lamps made from soda bottles, and some government offices were built in part with old telephone poles. The city also delivers excellent services, including a highly efficient bus system and well-constructed housing projects for the poor (Zwingle, 2002; Linden, 1993).

Most megacities fit between these two contrasting types. They are saddled with[6] serious problems but manage to cope reasonably well, usually in ways that reflect the nature of their societies. Consider Tokyo, for example—the world's most densely popu-lated metropolis. It faces enormous problems, such as overwhelming amounts of waste, traffic-choked streets, and sky-high housing costs. But the technologically advanced

[1]**collapse:** to fall down in a ruined condition
[2]**to be endowed with:** to naturally have a good quality
[3]**corrupt:** dishonest
[4]**loot:** to steal
[5]**inflation rate:** rise in prices
[6]**to be saddled with:** to struggle with

        Unit Two   Above material from: *Advanced Reading Power 4*

Japanese have, among other things, developed an urban heat system that extracts heat from sewage, which is then used to regulate the temperature in several of Tokyo's buildings. To reduce traffic jams, the city has used wireless communication to show drivers whose cars have a computerized navigation system where the congested[7] streets are. And to lower housing costs, Tokyo has started planning to build an underground city (Kuchment, 2003; Wehrfritz and Itoi, 2003; Linden, 1993).

[7]**congested:** crowded with traffic

Source: From Alex Thio, *Sociology: A Brief Introduction*, 6/e. Published by Allyn & Bacon, Boston, MA. © 2005 by Pearson Education. Reprinted by permission of the publisher.

c. *Compare your study question and text markings with those of another student. If you disagree, look back at the text to explain your work. Then write three quiz questions about this section.*

1. _____

2. _____

3. _____

d. *Ask another pair of students to answer your questions without looking back at the text. Then check the text for the answers.*

C. STRATEGY 3: CONNECTING GRAPHICS AND IDEAS

Textbooks and newspaper or magazine articles often use graphics to help make a point. These graphics can come in many different forms: graphs, charts, tables and diagrams. Always look at graphics carefully and connect them to specific parts of the text.

Example:
a. *Read this passage and study the graph showing the different ethnic backgrounds of millionaires in the United States. The underlined parts of the passage relate to the graph.*

THE TOP GROUPS OF U.S. MILLIONAIRES

The economic dominance of English Americans has faced vigorous <u>challenges from other European Americans,</u> who have rapidly moved up the ladder of success in business and other fields. Here is how <u>English Americans</u> compare with Americans of other European ancestries in percentage of <u>households having a net worth of $1 million or more.</u>

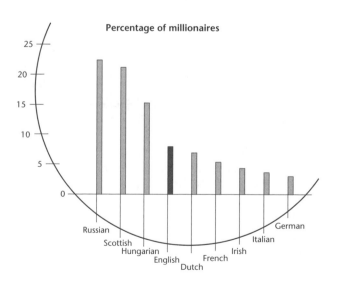

    b. Refer to the graph and the text to answer these questions.

       1. Which ethnic group has produced the fewest millionaires?

       2. Which has produced the most?

       3. Approximately how many millionaires are of Irish ancestry?

       4. Approximately how many are of English ancestry?

    c. Compare your work with that of another student. If you disagree, look back at the text and the graph and explain your work.

6. *a. Read this passage and study the graph showing differences in earnings for U.S. workers according to gender and ethnicity. Underline the parts of the passage that relate to the graph.*

Pay Levels for Women

    Despite protections, the earnings gap that many people see between the wages of men and women is only gradually being closed. Historically, this gap has been the result of social conditions for women. [. . .] Much progress has been made in creating job opportunities for women. Yet some qualified women still find that they cannot advance beyond a certain level in the companies they work for.

Pay Levels for Minorities

    Minorities tend to earn lower pay than whites do. In part, non-discrimination laws are designed to help minority workers get more access to job opportunities where they can improve their skills and build their experience. The goal is that over time these workers will be able to compete equally in the labor market and contribute more to the productive capacity of America.

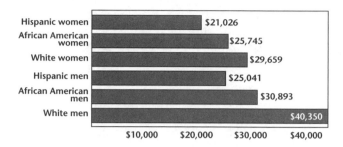

Median[1] Earnings for U.S. Workers, by Gender and Ethnicity, 2000

Source: U.S. Census Bureau

[1] **median:** the middle number in a set of numbers arranged in order

Source: Arthur O'Sullivan and Steven M. Sheffrin *Economics: Principles and Tools*, 2nd Edition. Upper Saddle River, NJ: Prentice Hall, 2003.

b. *Refer to the graph and the text to answer these questions.*

1. Which group has the lowest median earnings?

2. Which group has the highest median earnings?

3. Which group has higher median earnings—African American women or African American men?

4. Which group has higher median earnings—White women or Hispanic women?

c. *Compare your work with that of another student. If you disagree, look back at the text and the graph and explain your work.*

FOCUS ON VOCABULARY

1. a. *Check your understanding of the following target words. Read each word aloud and then write S, M, or N beside it.*

S = you are sure of the meaning of the word
M = you think you know the meaning of the word
N = you don't know the meaning of the word at all

_____ facilitate	_____ major	_____ pose
_____ virtually	_____ distinction	_____ construct
_____ core	_____ emergence	_____ extract
_____ adjacent	_____ collapse	_____ regulate

b. *Read the passages from Exercises 4 and 5 again. As you read, look for the target words and circle them. Note that the words in part a are listed in the same order as they appear in the passage, but the form may be different.*

Metropolis and Megalopolis

Early in this century, the large cities of the industrialized nations began to spread outward. They formed **metropolises**, large urban areas that include a city and its surrounding suburbs. Some of these suburbs are politically separate from their central cities, but socially, economically, and geographically, the suburbs and the city are tied together. The U.S. Census Bureau recognizes this unity by defining what is called a *Standard Metropolitan Statistical Area*, which cuts across political boundaries. Since 1990, most U.S. residents have been living in metropolitan areas with 1 million residents or more (Suro, 1991).

In the United States, the upper and middle classes have usually sparked the expansion of cities outward. Typically, as migrants from rural areas moved into the central city, the wealthier classes moved to the suburbs. The automobile greatly facilitated this development. It encouraged people to leave the crowded inner city for the more comfortable life of the suburbs, if they could afford it. As the number of cars increased, so did the size of suburbs and metropolises. In 1900, there were only 8,000 cars in the United States; by 1930, the number had soared to more than 26 million. Meanwhile, the proportion of the U.S. population living in the suburbs grew from only 15.7 percent in 1910 to 49.6 percent in 1950 (Glaab and Brown, 1983).

Since 1950, virtually all the growth in metropolitan areas has occurred in the suburbs. During the 1960s, U.S. suburbs grew four times faster than inner cities, and stores and entertainment facilities followed the people there. Suburban jobs increased 44 percent, while inner-city employment dropped 7 percent. This pattern of suburban growth at the expense of the urban core continued in the 1970s and 1980s. Today, suburbanites outnumber city residents three to two (U.S. Census Bureau, 2003; Gottdiener, 1983; Jaaret, 1983).

As suburbs expand, they sometimes combine with the suburbs of adjacent metropolitan areas to form a megalopolis, a vast area in which many metropolises merge. For hundreds of miles from one major city to the next, suburbs and cities have merged with one another to form a continuous region in which distinctions between suburban, urban, and rural areas are blurred. The hundreds of miles from Boston to Washington, D.C., form one such megalopolis; another stretches from Detroit through Chicago to Milwaukee in the Midwest; and a third goes from San Francisco to San Diego.

Unit Two   Above material from: *Advanced Reading Power 4*

The World's Megacities

The world's urban population has grown so fast that today, there are about 40 megacities—cities with populations of 5 million or more. Generally, the poorer the country, the faster its urban growth. Thus, today, only three of the world's megacities are in the United States, and more than half are in developing countries. Many more cities in the developing world will soon become megacities.1

Since the emergence of the pre-industrial city 5,000 years ago, great cities have risen and fallen. The same is true today. One city that is collapsing is Kinshasa, the capital of Zaire. Although the country is endowed with abundant natural resources, such as gold, diamonds, copper, and rich agricultural land, Kinshasa has produced massive miseries under the corrupt 30-year-reign of former President Sese Mobutu. Government officials have routinely looted manufactured goods, fuel, food, and medical supplies, even most of the emergency food aid sent by foreign countries. As a result, the annual inflation rate has often soared to more than 3,000 percent and the jobless rate to 80 percent, posing serious threats of starvation and epidemics. In contrast, the city of Curitiba in Brazil is a success story. The city is not rich, but its government makes the most of its resources. One example is recycling: Parks are lit with lamps made from soda bottles, and some government offices were built in part with old telephone poles. The city also delivers excellent services, including a highly efficient bus system and well-constructed housing projects for the poor (Zwingle, 2002; Linden, 1993).

Most megacities fit between these two contrasting types. They are saddled with serious problems but manage to cope reasonably well, usually in ways that reflect the nature of their societies. Consider Tokyo, for example—the world's most densely populated metropolis. It faces enormous problems, such as overwhelming amounts of waste, traffic-choked streets, and sky-high housing costs. But the technologically advanced Japanese have, among other things, developed an urban heat system that extracts heat from sewage, which is then used to regulate the temperature in several of Tokyo's buildings. To reduce traffic jams, the city has used wireless communication to show drivers whose cars have a computerized navigation system where the congested streets are. And to lower housing costs, Tokyo has started planning to build an underground city (Kuchment, 2003; Wehrfritz and Itoi, 2003; Linden, 1993).

Reprinted from *Sociology: A Brief Introduction*, Sixth Edition (2005), Allyn & Bacon, a Pearson Education Company.

Source: A. Thio, *Sociology: A Brief Introduction*, 6th Edition. Boston: Allyn and Bacon, 2005, p. 406–409.

    c. Working with another student, check to be sure that you have located all of the target words.

2. *a. These sentences are taken from the passages in Exercise 1. Working with another student, read each sentence aloud. Then circle the best meaning or synonym for the underlined word as it is used in the sentence.*

1. The automobile greatly <u>facilitated</u> this development.

    a. complicated

    b. put limits on

    c. made easier

2. Since 1950, <u>virtually</u> all the growth in metropolitan areas has occurred in the suburbs.

   a. almost

   b. probably

   c. entirely

3. This pattern of suburban growth at the expense of the urban <u>core</u> continued in the 1970s and 1980s.

   a. power

   b. economy

   c. center

4. As suburbs expand, they sometimes combine with the suburbs of <u>adjacent</u> metropolitan areas to form a megalopolis, a vast area in which many metropolises merge.

   a. large

   b. nearby

   c. distant

5. For hundreds of miles from one <u>major</u> city to the next, suburbs and cities have merged with one another to form a continuous region in which distinctions between suburban, urban, and rural areas are blurred.

   a. large

   b. growing

   c. wealthy

6. For hundreds of miles from one major city to the next, suburbs and cities have merged with one another to form a continuous region in which <u>distinctions</u> between suburban, urban, and rural areas are blurred.

   a. transportation

   b. differences

   c. similarities

7. Since the <u>emergence</u> of the pre-industrial city 5,000 years ago, great cities have risen and fallen.

   a. appearance

   b. disappearance

   c. end

Unit Two   Above material from: *Advanced Reading Power 4*

8. One city that is <u>collapsing</u> is Kinshasa, the capital of Zaire.

    a. starving

    b. growing

    c. failing

9. As a result, the annual inflation rate has often soared to more than 3,000 percent and the jobless rate to 80 percent, <u>posing</u> serious threats of starvation and epidemics.

    a. creating

    b. limiting

    c. avoiding

10. The city also delivers excellent services, including a highly efficient bus system and <u>well-constructed</u> housing projects for the poor.

    a. well-regarded

    b. well-built

    c. well-heated

11. But the technologically advanced Japanese have, among other things, developed an urban heat system that <u>extracts</u> heat from sewage, which is then used to regulate the temperature in several of Tokyo's buildings.

    a. removes

    b. preserves

    c. sends

12. But the technologically advanced Japanese have, among other things, developed an urban heat system that extracts heat from sewage, which is then used to <u>regulate</u> the temperature in several of Tokyo's buildings.

    a. support

    b. increase

    c. control

    b. *Compare your answers with those of another pair of students. If you disagree, explain your answer and then use a dictionary to check your work.*

3. *a. In this table, write as many of the missing forms as you can think of without looking in a dictionary.*

Noun	Verb	Adjective	Adverb
collapse			——
	construct		
core		——	——
distinction			
emergence			——
	extract		——
	facilitate		——
		major	——
	pose	——	——
	regulate		——
——	——		virtually

b. Compare your work with that of another student. Then look in the dictionary for the forms you did not know and write them in the table.

4. *a. Working with another student, write a form of one of the target words in each of the sentences below. Each word may be used only once.*

adjacent	distinction	major
collapse	emergence	pose
construct	extract	regulate
core	facilitate	virtually

1. According to the lawyer, it is necessary to make a _____ between the two cases, even if they seem similar at first glance.

2. The flow of water in the canal was _____ by the new flood gates that were installed before the storm.

3. In the United States and other developed countries, certain diseases like polio have _____ disappeared.

4. The journalist's question about the war _____ a serious political problem for the president.

5. The new traffic rules will _____ the flow of traffic around the city.

6. George Bernard Shaw was a _____ influence on the theater in the twentieth century.

Unit Two   Above material from: *Advanced Reading Power 4*

7. Italy _____ from the war with its industry and transportation systems in a very poor state.

8. When the Eiffel Tower was _____ in the late nineteenth century, it was considered a marvel of engineering.

9. Although the acting and the filming is excellent, the real _____ of the film is its political message.

10. The chemistry laboratory is located in the building that is _____ to the library.

11. When the housing market _____ and the prices of houses fell, some people were in serious financial difficulty.

12. Many art museums now have machines that _____ the humidity (water) from the air.

   b. *Compare your answers with those of another pair of students. If you disagree, explain your answers and look back at the passage to check your work. You may also use a dictionary to check your work.*

5. a. *Make study cards for the target words that you are still unsure about. Use the cards to study them, first on your own and then with another student.*

   b. 1. Write a sentence for each of the words, leaving a blank instead of the target word. Ask another student to read your sentences and write the target word that should go in each blank.

   2. Look at your sentences again. If your classmate wrote a different word, discuss the sentences to find out why. Was your sentence unclear, or did your classmate not know the target word?

Unit Three

Reading for Integrated Skills Tasks

Bill Gates

A. PREVIEWING THE ACADEMIC CONTENT

What characteristics make Bill Gates, the founder of Microsoft, so successful? Successful businesspeople have always fascinated the public and researchers alike. Researchers have studied successful business leaders to develop theories that explain their successes. What qualities do they have, how do they behave, and does their behavior change depending on the work situation?

1. *Here is a list of qualities that might be valuable in a leader. Rate them from most important (1) to least important (11). Then compare your ranking with another student's. Are there differences in your rankings? Explain why you ranked these qualities in the order you did by giving examples from your own experience.*

_____ Charismatic—motivates people by inspiring them

_____ Directive—gives direction to others

_____ Ruthless—demonstrates determination when making unpleasant decisions

_____ Sensitive—understands others' problems

_____ Communicative—communicates key information

_____ Cunning—uses clever but possibly dishonest means to achieve a goal

_____ Team builder—facilitates groups of employees working together to achieve a goal

_____ Intelligent—thinks clearly and understands quickly

_____ Organized—plans ahead to ensure needs are met

_____ Self-monitoring—considers how to work more efficiently

_____ Persevering—continuing in spite of difficulties

What other qualities can you add to this list?

B. PREVIEWING THE ACADEMIC SKILLS FOCUS

Most academic texts are expository in nature, that is, they are written to provide information. As you read books and articles and listen to lectures, you will discover that the texts are often organized in similar patterns. Recognizing patterns of organization can help you predict and anticipate what you will read or hear next, which can make your reading faster and your listening easier.

What are patterns of organization? You may be familiar with some of them already. Typical patterns of text organization are description, definition, process, cause-effect, advantage-disadvantage, problem-solution, and compare-contrast. These patterns are closely linked to an author's purpose.

Patterns of Organization	Author's Purpose
Description text	Describe someone or something
Definition text	Define a term and give an example
Process text	Explain how to do something
Cause-effect text	Explain what caused something
Advantages-disadvantages text	List the strengths and weaknesses of something
Problem-solution text	Describe a problem and explain a solution
Compare and/or contrast text	Show similarities or differences between two or more items

Work with a partner. Read the text outlines. Label each outline with the correct pattern of organization: description, definition, process, cause-effect, advantages-disadvantages, problem-solution, or compare-contrast. Then check your answers with the class. What might explain any differences you have?

a. Organizational Pattern: _____ *Description text* _____

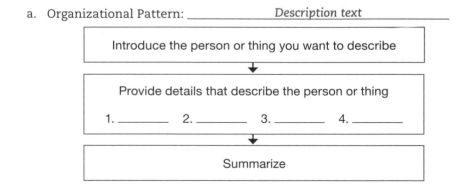

b. Organizational Pattern: _____

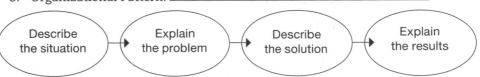

c. Organizational Pattern: _____

Block-Style Organization		**Point-by-Point Organization**	
Introduce two items		Introduce two items	
Describe item 1 1.	Describe item 2 1.	Point 1	Describe item 1 Describe item 2
2.	2.	Point 2	Describe item 1 Describe item 2
3.	3.	Point 3	Describe item 1 Describe item 2
Conclusion		Conclusion	

d. Organizational Pattern: _____

| Introduce the term to be defined | is a | Classify the term | that | Provide a definition |

e. Organizational Pattern: _____

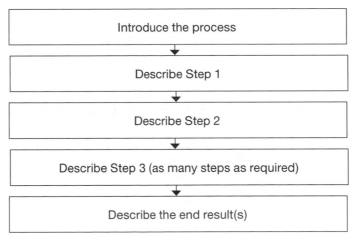

Introduce the process

↓

Describe Step 1

↓

Describe Step 2

↓

Describe Step 3 (as many steps as required)

↓

Describe the end result(s)

f. Organizational Pattern: _____

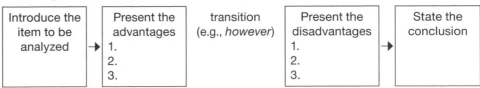

| Introduce the item to be analyzed | → | Present the advantages
1.
2.
3. | transition (e.g., *however*) | Present the disadvantages
1.
2.
3. | → | State the conclusion |

g. Organizational Pattern: _____

| Describe the cause | → | Describe the effect |

C. BEFORE YOU READ

1. *Work in small groups. Read the paragraphs and answer the questions.*

Boss A

You have just been hired by a small company that sells computer parts. You will be the receptionist for the company, directing phone calls to the appropriate salespeople, taking phone messages, greeting visitors, and so on. This is your first job, and you are very nervous. Your boss meets you a little early on your first day and shows you your desk and phone. You admit to being nervous. Your boss is encouraging and says, "Don't worry, you'll be fine. It's good to be nervous on the first day. In a few days, you'll feel right at home." She then wishes you good luck and leaves. The phone starts to ring, and the first visitors come through the door. You realize you don't know the names or phone extensions of the salespeople, or how to work the complicated phone system.

Boss B

You have just been hired by a small photocopying company. As you don't have much customer service experience, you will spend most of your time photocopying the orders that the customer service representatives take. Your boss meets you a little early on the first day. He shows you the photocopier you will be using, how to change the paper and the copy settings, and where the ink cartridges are located. He has three large photocopy jobs for you this morning. He says you must finish the three large jobs before lunch or you will be fired, and he goes away.

personal quality =
characteristic =
trait

1. *List the traits each boss demonstrates. Then discuss which boss you would rather work for and why.*

2. *Do you think that knowing the boss's traits will tell you if he or she is someone you would want to work for? What other things about a boss or the company might help you decide if you would want to work there?*

2. *With your group, discuss each vocabulary item and its meaning in the chart below. Then complete the third column to link the new vocabulary to your own experience.*

Vocabulary Item	Meaning	Link to Your Own Experience
1. implicit assumption	Something that is understood without being stated	Give an example of an implicit assumption. *Education is good.* Can you think of others?
2. stable personality	A personality that is steady, reliable, and not changeable	Name someone famous who has a stable personality.
3. orchestrate a turnaround	To organize, arrange, and manage a complete change in fortune or outcome	Name a politician who has orchestrated a turnaround of a country.
4. ailing company/ ailing person	A company that is not doing well / A person in poor health	Give an example of an ailing company or an ailing person.

Vocabulary Item	Meaning	Link to Your Own Experience
5. extroversion	A personality characteristic of someone who is confident and enjoys the company of others	Name someone you know who has an extroverted personality.
6. prominent firm	A company that is doing well in business	Name five prominent firms.
7. the former . . . the latter	*The former* refers to the idea or point that comes first in a sentence, and *the latter* refers to the idea or point that comes second in a sentence.	In the sentence below, which idea is the former, and which one is the latter? *While motivational leaders inspire their employees to do well, directive leaders risk annoying their employees by sounding bossy.* Which type of leader would you rather work for, the former or the latter?

D. GLOBAL READING

1. Recognizing Multiple Organizational Patterns

Short texts, like the ones you have looked at so far in this unit, usually demonstrate only a single pattern of organization. However, when you read or listen to longer texts, you may notice that longer texts are often divided into sections, and each section may have its own organizational pattern. This is the case with the textbook excerpt you will read in this section.

2. *Read the text. Work alone to determine the pattern of organization for each section of the text. Write it in the space provided. Then discuss your answers with the class.*

THE SEARCH FOR LEADERSHIP TRAITS

1   Throughout history, social observers have been fascinated by obvious demonstrations of successful interpersonal influence, whether the consequences of this influence were good, bad, or mixed. Individuals such as Henry Ford, Martin Luther King, Jr., Barbara Jordan, Ralph Nader, and Joan of Arc have been analyzed and reanalyzed to discover what made them leaders and what set them apart from less successful leaders. The implicit assumption here is that those who become leaders and do a good job of it possess a special set of traits that distinguishes them from the masses of followers. While philosophers and the popular media have advocated such a position for centuries, trait theories of leadership did not receive serious scientific attention until the 1900s.

2   During World War I the U.S. military recognized that it had a leadership problem. Never before had the country mounted such a massive war effort, and able officers were in short supply. Thus, the search for leadership traits that might be useful in identifying potential officers began. Following the war, and continuing through World War II, this interest expanded to include searching for leadership traits in populations as diverse as schoolchildren and business executives. Some

studies tried to differentiate traits of leaders and followers, while others searched for traits that predicted leader effectiveness or distinguished lower-level leaders from higher-level leaders.

Organizational pattern for paragraphs 1 and 2: _cause-effect or a short_

problem-solution text

3   Just what is a trait, anyway? **Traits** are personal characteristics of an individual that include physical characteristics, intellectual ability, and personality. Research has shown that many traits are not associated with whether people become leaders or how effective they are. However, research also shows that some traits are associated with leadership. Exhibit 1 provides a list of these traits. As you might expect, leaders (or more successful leaders) tend to be higher than average on these dimensions, although the connections are not very strong. Notice that the list portrays a high-energy person who really wants to have an impact on others but at the same time

Paul Tellier

is smart and stable enough not to abuse his or her power. Interestingly, this is a very accurate summary description of Bombardier CEO Paul Tellier, who, while CEO of Canadian National Railways, orchestrated a turnaround that transformed the ailing company into the best run and most efficient railroad in North America.

Exhibit 1
Traits associated with leadership effectiveness.

Traits.   Individual characteristics such as physical attributes, intellectual ability, and personality

Intelligence
Energy
Self-confidence
Dominance
Motivation to lead
Emotional stability
Honesty and integrity
Need for achievement

Organizational pattern for paragraph 3: _____

4   In recent years, there has been a renewed interest in the study of leadership traits, and a number of studies have shown that certain traits are more closely linked to leadership. For example, one study found that three of the "Big Five" dimensions of personality (agreeableness, extraversion, and openness to experience) are related to leadership behaviors. In addition, research that compared top performers with average performers in senior leadership positions found that the most effective leaders have high levels of emotional intelligence. The emotional intelligence of leaders has also been found to be positively related to the job satisfaction and organizational citizenship behavior of employees. Many prominent firms use personality tests and assessment centers to measure leadership traits when making hiring and promotion decisions. However, there are some aspects of the trait approach that limit its ultimate usefulness.

Unit Three   Above material from: *Academic Connections 4*

5   Even though some traits appear to be related to leadership, there are several reasons why the trait approach is not the best means of understanding and improving leadership. In many cases, it is difficult to determine whether traits make the leader or whether the opportunity for leadership produces the traits. For example, do dominant individuals tend to become leaders, or do employees become more dominant *after* they successfully occupy leadership roles? This distinction is important. If the former is true, we might wish to seek out dominant people and appoint them to leadership roles. If the latter is true, this strategy will not work. Secondly, even if we know that dominance, intelligence, or tallness is associated with effective leadership, we have few clues about what dominant or intelligent or tall people *do* to influence others successfully. As a result, we have little information about how to train and develop leaders and no way to diagnose failures of leadership. And finally, the most crucial problem of the trait approach to leadership is its failure to take into account the *situation* in which leadership occurs. Intuitively, it seems reasonable that top executives and first-level supervisors might require different traits to be successful. Similarly, physical prowess might be useful in directing a logging crew but irrelevant to managing a team of scientists.

6   In summary, although there are some traits that are associated with leadership success, traits alone are not sufficient for successful leadership. Traits are only a pre-condition for certain actions that a leader must take in order to be successful. In other words, possessing the appropriate traits for leadership makes it possible—and even more likely—that certain actions will be taken and will be successful.

Source: Johns, G. & Saks, A.M. (2005). *Organizational behavior: Understanding and managing life at work* (6th ed.). Toronto: Pearson Prentice Hall.

Organizational pattern for paragraphs 4, 5, and 6: _____

3. *Complete the graphic organizers to show the organization of the content of this reading.*

Paragraphs 1 and 2

What *caused* the interest in trait theory?	What was the *effect* of this interest?
_____ _____ _____	_____ _____ _____

Paragraph 3

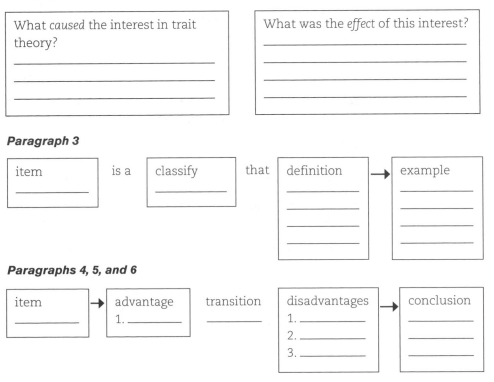

Paragraphs 4, 5, and 6

4. *Work with a partner to answer the questions.*

1. What is the assumption about why some people become leaders and others do not?

2. Why did researchers begin to study leadership traits, and why was it important at that time?

3. What is a trait?

4. What are some traits that are associated with successful leaders?

5. What are the three weaknesses of the trait theory *that the author writes about?* Check (✓) your answers.

_____ trait theory doesn't reflect a modern way of thinking

_____ trait theory doesn't explain which comes first, the leadership traits or the leadership position

_____ trait theory doesn't explain why some people with leadership traits aren't leaders

_____ trait theory doesn't explain how leaders behave or what they do

_____ trait theory doesn't explain how leaders behave in different situations

_____ trait theory doesn't help identify the soldiers that make good leaders

E. Focused Reading

1. Recognizing Relationships among Ideas in a Text

Just as recognizing organizational patterns of a text helps you read faster or listen better, recognizing connecting words in a text can help you understand the relationships among ideas. Here are some key connecting words.

- *To introduce points, examples, and reasons, a writer/speaker may use* first, second, next, finally, for example, *and* such as.

Example

First, trait theory was used to identify potentially successful leaders.

- *To show the addition of another point, a writer/speaker may use* in addition, furthermore, *and* moreover *to join clauses or sentences.*

Examples

Trait theory did not succeed at predicting leadership success; *in addition*, it failed to demonstrate if the traits preceded success or success preceded the traits.

Trait theory did not succeed at predicting leadership success. *Moreover*, it failed to demonstrate if the traits preceded success or success preceded the traits.

- *To show a result, a writer/speaker may use* so *to join two clauses and* as a result, therefore, thus, *and* consequently *to join clauses or sentences together.*

Examples

Trait theory did not explain all the questions researchers had about leader success, *so* psychologists turned to behavior theory.

Behavior theory did not take into account how the work situation affected the leader's behavior; *as a result*, researchers began to consider situational theory.

Behavior theory did not take into account how the work situation affected the leader's behavior. *Therefore*, researchers began to consider situational theory.

- **To show contrast**, *a writer/speaker may use* while, although, even though, *or* whereas *to join an adverb clause and an independent clause*. However *or* on the other hand *may be used to join clauses or sentences*.

Examples

While trait theory identified potential leaders, behavioral theory explained how leaders behaved when they were in a job.

Some traits are associated with leadership success; *however*, some traits are obviously not.

- *A writer/speaker may also* **show contrast** *by using* but *to join two independent clauses.*

Example

Trait theory showed promise to explain leadership success, *but* the theory also had weaknesses that could not be overcome.

- **To show similarity,** *a writer/speaker may use* similarly *or* likewise *to join clauses or sentences.*

Example

Some leaders are noted for their charisma; *similarly*, these leaders are often skillful communicators.

- **To conclude** *a text, a writer/speaker may use* in conclusion, in summary, *or* in closing.

Example

In summary, both trait and behavioral theory have their limitations.

The words that show the relationships among the ideas in the text have been omitted. Fill in each blank with an appropriate word to show the relationships (in parentheses) between the ideas. Compare your answers with a classmate's, and then check the answers against the original reading. Your answers may be different from those in the reading.

1. Throughout history, social observers have been fascinated by obvious demonstrations of successful interpersonal influence, whether the consequences of this influence were good, bad, or mixed. Individuals _____ (give examples) Henry Ford, Martin Luther King, Jr., Barbara Jordan, Ralph Nader, and Joan of Arc have been analyzed and reanalyzed to discover what made them leaders and what set them apart from less successful leaders.

2. _____ (show contrast) philosophers and the popular media have advocated such a position for centuries, trait theories of leadership did not receive serious scientific attention until the 1900s.

3. During World War I the U.S. military recognized that it had a leadership problem. Never before had the country mounted such a massive war effort, and able officers were in short supply. _____, (show a result) the search for leadership traits that might be useful in identifying potential officers began.

4. Research has shown that many traits are not associated with whether people become leaders or how effective they are. _____, (show contrast) research also shows that some traits are associated with leadership.

5. As you might expect, leaders (or more successful leaders) tend to be higher than average on these dimensions, _____ (show contrast) the connections are not very strong.

6. For example, one study found that three of the "Big Five" dimensions of personality (agreeableness, extraversion, and openness to experience) are related to leadership behaviors. _____, (add a point) research that compared top performers with average performers in senior leadership positions found that the most effective leaders have high levels of emotional intelligence.

7. Secondly, even if we know that dominance, intelligence, or tallness is associated with effective leadership, we have few clues about what dominant or intelligent or tall people do to influence others successfully. _____, (show a result) we have little information about how to train and develop leaders and no way to diagnose failures of leadership.

8. _____, (conclude) although there are some traits that are associated with leadership success, traits alone are not sufficient for successful leadership.

F. BEFORE YOU LISTEN

Work with a partner. Check the correct column to show whether a leader's behavior is an example of consideration behavior or initiation behavior. Then discuss your answers with the class.

consideration behavior *exp* leadership behavior that builds trust, respect, and good relationships with employees

initiation behavior *exp* leadership behavior that makes employees work efficiently

Leader's Behavior	Consideration Behaviors	Initiation Behaviors
1. assigning an employee a task to complete		✓
2. celebrating the birthdays of employees	✓	
3. complimenting an employee who has performed well		
4. setting short-term productivity goals for a team		
5. calculating the number of unhappy customers to show employees where customer service needs to improve		
6. giving a lunch for employees and their families		
7. spending a few minutes each day to find out how employees are doing		
8. setting long-term goals for company productivity		
9. asking employees for their opinions before beginning a new project		
10. making a controversial decision without asking employees for their opinions		

G. GLOBAL LISTENING

1. Organizing Information

Organizing information can help you in a number of ways. It can help you

- *see the relationships between/among ideas*
- *reduce large amounts of information into smaller chunks*
- *remember the information*
- *prepare to present information*

2. Organizational Tools

When you organize information, you can use a variety of tools to help you. You can use these three common tools:

- *graphic organizers*
- *charts*
- *outlines*

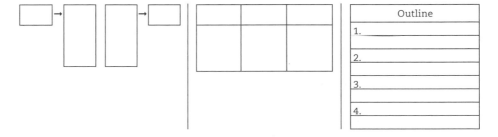

3. Lecture Organization

When you are thinking about the organization of a lecture, remember that most academic lectures have an introduction, a body, and a conclusion. The introduction can be very short but is key to understanding the organization of the lecture. In the *introduction*, the instructor may

- *review information from a previous lecture or reading*
- *introduce a new broad topic*
- *narrow the broader topic to a specific topic*

In the *body* of the lecture, the instructor will continue by providing information about the topic. This information may be organized into patterns with which you are already familiar:

- *description—to describe someone or something*
- *definition—to define a term*
- *process—to explain how to do something*
- *cause and effect—to explain what caused something*
- *advantages-disadvantages—to list the strengths and weaknesses of something*
- *problem-solution—to describe a problem and explain a solution*
- *compare and/or contrast—to show similarities and/or differences*

The *conclusion* can be very short but is key to knowing what to do before the next lecture. In the conclusion of the lecture, the instructor may

- *mention the topic of the next lecture*
- *tell students the homework for the next day*

4. *These 10 key pieces of information from the lecture are listed out of order. Place each piece of information in the appropriate place in the lecture outline.*

Key Pieces of Lecture Information

1. ~~Review of trait theory~~

2. Homework: to read about situational theories of leadership

3. Introduction to behavioral theory

4. An example of consideration versus initiation behavior

5. ~~Research on behavioral theory~~

6. Weakness of behavioral theory

7. Weakness of trait theory

8. Research on the influence of work situations

9. Two main orientations of behavioral theory: consideration and initiation behaviors—definitions

10. Work situations and their impact on leadership behavior

Leadership Behavior

Date: _____

Lecture Outline for Behavioral Theories of Leadership

Introduction:

1. *Review of trait theory* _____

2. _____

Body:

3. _____

4. *Research on behavioral theory* _____

5. _____

6. _____

7. _____

8. _____

9. _____

Conclusion:

10. _____

---

5. 🎧 *Listen to the lecture to check the order of the information. Then confirm the order with the class.*

6. *Use your notes in the outline above and your memory of the content of the lecture to answer the questions. If necessary, listen to the lecture again. Then compare your answers with a classmate's.*

1. What were the two orientations of the behavioral theory of leadership discovered by researchers at Ohio State University? Give an example of each.

2. What was the weakness of the behavioral theory of leadership?

3. Classify the characteristics of a work situation (shown in the box) into two categories: characteristics that create stress and characteristics that don't create stress. When you have finished, decide which leader behavior (consideration or initiation) is best for each situation. Discuss your answers with the class.

clearly defined task	long lead time (lots of time before a deadline)
experienced employees	tight deadlines
inexperienced employees	unclear task

Characteristics of Work Situations that Create Stress	**Characteristics of Work Situations that Don't Create Stress**
Most effective leader behavior for these situations:	Most effective leader behavior for these situations:

H. FOCUSED LISTENING

1. Recognizing Relationships among Parts of a Lecture

You may remember from the Reading section that brief reading texts usually demonstrate one pattern of organization, and longer readings may demonstrate multiple patterns of organization. Similarly, brief lectures usually demonstrate only one pattern of organization, and longer lectures may demonstrate multiple patterns of organization. For a longer lecture, listen for the same kinds of connecting words that you see in a longer reading text to help identify the patterns of organization within the lecture.

2. *Classify the words from the box into the appropriate columns to help you remember the words that indicate relationships among parts of a lecture.*

although	however	on the other hand
as a result	in addition	second
but	in closing	similarly
consequently	in conclusion	so
even though	in contrast	such as
finally	in summary	therefore
~~first~~	likewise	thus
for example	moreover	whereas
furthermore	next	~~while~~

To Introduce Points, Examples, Reasons	To Add a Point	To Show a Result	To Show a Contrast	To Show a Similarity	To Conclude
first			*while*		

The lecture is a good example of a problem-solution text that repeats itself. Remember that a traditional problem-solution text consists of four parts: situation, problem, solution, and results.

3. *Listen again to the lecture. In the first column of the chart, write the connecting words that indicate the relationships among the parts of the lecture.*

Words that Show Relationships among Ideas	Content	Pattern of Organization
To start,	Review of trait theory	Stage one: situation
	Trait theory was useful to describe leaders, but which came first, the traits or the leader?	Stage two: problem
	Behavioral theory	Stage three: solution
	Consideration and initiating behaviors	Short definition text
	Example of David Pottruck	Stage one: situation
	Employees didn't like working with Pottruck	Stage two: problem

Words that Show Relationships among Ideas	Content	Pattern of Organization
	Pottruck changed his leadership style	Stage three: solution
	Employees began to like working with Pottruck and now cooperate with him	Stage four: results
	Behavior theory weakness—the situation often affects the behavior of the leader	Stage two: problem
	Researchers began to consider the impact of work situation	Stage three: solution
	Work situation is important, so leaders should consider it, too	Stage four: not revealed

I. INTEGRATED WRITING TASK

Translate IT is a software company that has developed a product that translates text from one language to another. You will read about a leadership problem at Translate IT and discuss the problem with a small group of students. You will then develop a written response to the problem on your own.

1. *Read the explanation of the work situation at Translate IT. Then work in small groups to answer the questions.*

THE LEADERSHIP PROBLEM AT TRANSLATE IT

You are the founding entrepreneur and CEO of Translate IT, a fast-growing digital software company that specializes in translation software. Customer demand to license your software has boomed so much that in just two years you have added over 50 new software programmers to help develop a new range of software products. These people are young and inexperienced but are highly skilled and used to putting in long hours to see their ideas succeed. The growth of the company has been so swift that you still operate informally. As CEO, you have been so absorbed in your own work that you have paid little attention to the issue of leading your growing company. You have allowed your programmers to find solutions to problems as they go. They have also been allowed to form their own work groups, but there are signs that problems are arising.

There have been increasing complaints from employees that you do not recognize or reward good performance and that they do not feel equitably treated. Moreover, there have been growing concerns that top managers are either too busy or not willing to listen to the employees' new ideas and act on them. A bad atmosphere seems to be developing in the company, and recently several talented programmers have left.

As the CEO, you realize that you have done a poor job of leading your employees and that you need to develop a leadership approach to encourage workers to perform well and to stay with your company.

Source: Based on George, J.M., & Jones, G.R. (2005). *Understanding and managing organizational behavior* (4th ed.). Upper Saddle River, NJ: Pearson Prentice Hall.

1. What advantages does Translate IT have?

2. What challenges does Translate IT have?

3. As the CEO, what traits do you need in order to orchestrate a company turnaround? Why?

4. What leader behavior orientation would work best at Translate IT? Why?

5. What management style have you been using? What management style might work best now?

6. What solutions will you try to orchestrate a turnaround at Translate IT?

2. *Prepare a written presentation in which you explain how you will orchestrate a turnaround at Translate IT. Follow the steps to prepare your presentation.*

Step 1

Before you write, it is best to plan the information on which you will write. Use the connecting words you learned in the Reading and the Listening sections to signal the relationships between (or among) the pieces of information. To prepare, organize the information on which you will need to write in the chart. Most of the information you need is found in the answers to questions 1–6 above. Start your response with an introduction to the leadership problem. In your body paragraphs, state how these problems come about and the result of these problems. Then conclude with the solutions you will use to orchestrate the company's turnaround.

Organizational Chart	
Introduction to the leadership problems at Translate IT	
The advantages of Translate IT	
Key sentence or connecting word	
The challenges of Translate IT	
Necessary leadership traits	
Most effective behavior orientation	
Key sentence or connecting word	
Best managerial style	
Key sentence or connecting word	
Solutions	

Step 2

Use your notes to present your response to a partner. Then listen as your partner presents his or her response to you.

Unit Three   Above material from: *Academic Connections 4*

Unit Four
Reading Fiction

A. Katherine Mansfield (1888–1923)

Born in Wellington, New Zealand, Katherine Mansfield was the daughter of a wealthy businessman and a cold, sickly mother. In 1908, determined to become a writer, she left for London, where she adopted a highly unconventional lifestyle while relishing the city's intellectual stimulation. She married twice, bore a child out of wedlock, and became a close friend of D. H. Lawrence. She was at the height of her literary powers when she was diagnosed with tuberculosis in 1918.

During her life, Mansfield worked tirelessly to refine the technique of impressionist writing. Ironically, she was to find almost all the material she needed for her stories in her early life with her family in New Zealand. She drew on her past for many of her themes, especially those that highlighted the price paid by a woman in marriage and the plight of a woman on her own in an unfriendly world.

Mansfield's volumes of short stories include *In a German Pension* (1911), *Prelude* (1918), *Bliss and Other Stories* (1923), and *Stories by Katherine Mansfield* (1930).

Miss Brill

A lonely woman enjoys her Sunday afternoon outings to the park until her encounter with a thoughtless young couple.

Although it was so brilliantly fine—the blue sky powdered with gold and great spots of light like white wine splashed over the Jardins Publiques[1]—Miss Brill was glad that she had decided on her fur. The air was motionless, but when you opened your mouth there was just a faint chill, like a chill from a glass of iced water before you
5   sip, and now and again a leaf came drifting[2]—from nowhere, from the sky. Miss Brill put up her hand and touched her fur. Dear little thing! It was nice to feel it again. She had taken it out of its box that afternoon, shaken out the moth-powder, given it a good brush, and rubbed the life back into the dim little eyes. "What has been happening to me?" said the sad little eyes. Oh, how sweet it was to see them snap at
10   her again from the red eiderdown![3] . . . But the nose, which was of some black composition, wasn't at all firm. It must have had a knock, somehow. Never mind—a

---

[1]**Jardins Publiques**: Public Gardens (French)
[2]**drifting**: floating down
[3]**eiderdown**: a warm bed cover

little dab of black sealing-wax[4] when the time came—when it was absolutely necessary. . . . Little rogue![5] Yes, she really felt like that about it. Little rogue biting its tail just by her left ear. She could have taken it off and laid it on her lap and
15 stroked it. She felt a tingling[6] in her hands and arms, but that came from walking, she supposed. And when she breathed, something light and sad—no, not sad, exactly—something gentle seemed to move in her bosom.

There were a number of people out this afternoon, far more than last Sunday. And the band sounded louder and gayer.[7] That was because the Season had begun.
20 For although the band played all the year round on Sundays, out of season[8] it was never the same. It was like some one playing with only the family to listen; it didn't care how it played if there weren't any strangers present. Wasn't the conductor wearing a new coat, too? She was sure it was new. He scraped with his foot and flapped his arms like a rooster about to crow,[9] and the bandsmen sitting in the green
25 rotunda[10] blew out their cheeks and glared at the music. Now there came a little "flutey"[11] bit—very pretty!—a little chain of bright drops. She was sure it would be repeated. It was; she lifted her head and smiled.

Only two people shared her "special" seat: a fine old man in a velvet coat, his hands clasped over a huge carved walking-stick, and a big old woman, sitting
30 upright, with a roll of knitting on her embroidered apron. They did not speak. This was disappointing, for Miss Brill always looked forward to the conversation. She had become really quite expert, she thought, at listening as though she didn't listen, at sitting in other people's lives just for a minute while they talked round her.

She glanced, sideways, at the old couple. Perhaps they would go soon. Last
35 Sunday, too, hadn't been as interesting as usual. An Englishman and his wife, he wearing a dreadful Panama hat[12] and she button boots. And she'd gone on[13] the whole time about how she ought to wear spectacles; she knew she needed them; but that it was no good getting any; they'd be sure to break and they'd never keep on. And he'd been so patient. He'd suggested everything—gold rims, the kind that
40 curved round your ears, little pads inside the bridge. No, nothing would please her. "They'll always be sliding down my nose!" Miss Brill had wanted to shake her.

The old people sat on the bench, still as statues. Never mind, there was always the crowd to watch. To and fro,[14] in front of the flower-beds and the band rotunda, the couples and groups paraded, stopped to talk, to greet, to buy a handful of flow-
45 ers from the old beggar who had his tray fixed to the railings. Little children ran among them, swooping[15] and laughing; little boys with big white silk bows under their chins, little girls, little French dolls, dressed up in velvet and lace. And sometimes a tiny staggerer[16] came suddenly rocking into the open from under the trees, stopped, stared, as suddenly sat down "flop," until its small high-stepping mother,

[4]**dab of black sealing-wax**: a tiny amount of black patching material
[5]**rogue**: a mischievous person
[6]**tingling**: a prickly sensation
[7]**gayer**: happier
[8]**out of season**: socially, during the less important months
[9]**about to crow**: getting ready to make a rooster's cry
[10]**rotunda**: a round building covered by a dome
[11]**"flutey"**: like a flute (usually spelled *fluty*)
[12]**Panama hat**: a lightweight straw hat
[13]**gone on**: talked endlessly
[14]**To and fro**: Forward and backward
[15]**swooping**: moving downward quickly
[16]**staggerer**: someone who moves very unsteadily

50 like a young hen, rushed scolding[17] to its rescue. Other people sat on the benches and green chairs, but they were nearly always the same, Sunday after Sunday, and—Miss Brill had often noticed—there was something funny about nearly all of them. They were odd, silent, nearly all old, and from the way they stared they looked as though they'd just come from dark little rooms or even—even cupboards![18]

55   Behind the rotunda the slender trees with yellow leaves down drooping, and through them just a line of sea, and beyond the blue sky with gold-veined clouds.

    Tum-tum-tum tiddle-um! tiddle-um! tum tiddley-um tum ta! blew the band.

    Two young girls in red came by and two young soldiers in blue met them, and they laughed and paired and went off arm-in-arm. Two peasant women with funny

60 straw hats passed, gravely, leading beautiful smoke-coloured donkeys. A cold, pale nun hurried by. A beautiful woman came along and dropped her bunch of violets, and a little boy ran after to hand them to her, and she took them and threw them away as if they'd been poisoned. Dear me! Miss Brill didn't know whether to admire that or not! And now an ermine toque[19] and a gentleman in grey met just in front of

65 her. He was tall, stiff, dignified, and she was wearing the ermine toque she'd bought when her hair was yellow. Now everything, her hair, her face, even her eyes, was the same colour as the shabby[20] ermine, and her hand, in its cleaned glove, lifted to dab her lips, was a tiny yellowish paw. Oh, she was so pleased to see him—delighted! She rather thought they were going to meet that afternoon. She described where she'd

70 been—everywhere, here, there, along by the sea. The day was so charming—didn't he agree? And wouldn't he, perhaps? . . . But he shook his head, lighted a cigarette, slowly breathed a great deep puff into her face, and, even while she was still talking and laughing, flicked the match away and walked on. The ermine toque was alone; she smiled more brightly than ever. But even the band seemed to know what she

75 was feeling and played more softly, played tenderly, and the drum beat, "The Brute! The Brute!" over and over. What would she do? What was going to happen now? But as Miss Brill wondered, the ermine toque turned, raised her hand as though she'd seen some one else, much nicer, just over there, and pattered[21] away. And the band changed again and played more quickly, more gaily than ever, and the old couple

80 on Miss Brill's seat got up and marched away, and such a funny old man with long whiskers[22] hobbled[23] along in time to the music and was nearly knocked over by four girls walking abreast.[24]

    Oh, how fascinating it was! How she enjoyed it! How she loved sitting here, watching it all! It was like a play. It was exactly like a play. Who could believe the sky

85 at the back wasn't painted? But it wasn't till a little brown dog trotted on solemn and then slowly trotted off, like a little "theatre" dog, a little dog that had been drugged, that Miss Brill discovered what it was that made it so exciting. They were all on the stage. They weren't only the audience, not only looking on; they were acting. Even she had a part and came every Sunday. No doubt somebody would have noticed if

90 she hadn't been there; she was part of the performance after all. How strange she'd

---

[17]**scolding**: expressing disapproval
[18]**cupboards**: closets
[19]**ermine toque**: a small, close-fitting woman's hat made of the fur of an ermine, a small white animal
[20]**shabby**: worn and old-looking
[21]**pattered**: ran with light, quick steps
[22]**whiskers**: a beard or sometimes a mustache
[23]**hobbled**: walked with great difficulty
[24]**walking abreast**: walking side by side

never thought of it like that before! And yet it explained why she made such a point of[25] starting from home at just the same time each week—so as not to be late for the performance—and it also explained why she had quite a queer, shy feeling at telling her English pupils how she spent her Sunday afternoons. No wonder! Miss
95 Brill nearly laughed out loud. She was on the stage. She thought of the old invalid[26] gentleman to whom she read the newspaper four afternoons a week while he slept in the garden. She had got quite used to the frail head on the cotton pillow, the hollowed eyes, the open mouth and the high pinched[27] nose. If he'd been dead she mightn't have noticed for weeks; she wouldn't have minded. But suddenly he knew
100 he was having the paper read to him by an actress! "An actress!" The old head lifted; two points of light quivered in the old eyes. "An actress—are ye?" And Miss Brill smoothed the newspaper as though it were the manuscript of her part and said gently: "Yes, I have been an actress for a long time."

The band had been having a rest. Now they started again. And what they played
105 was warm, sunny, yet there was just a faint chill—a something, what was it?—not sadness—no, not sadness—a something that made you want to sing. The tune lifted, lifted, the light shone; and it seemed to Miss Brill that in another moment all of them, all the whole company, would begin singing. The young ones, the laughing ones who were moving together, they would begin, and the men's voices, very
110 resolute and brave, would join them. And then she too, she too, and the others on the benches—they would come in with a kind of accompaniment—something low, that scarcely rose or fell, something so beautiful—moving. . . . And Miss Brill's eyes filled with tears and she looked smiling at all the other members of the company. Yes, we understand, we understand, she thought—though what they understood
115 she didn't know.

Just at that moment a boy and girl came and sat down where the old couple had been. They were beautifully dressed; they were in love. The hero and heroine, of course, just arrived from his father's yacht.[28] And still soundlessly singing, still with that trembling smile, Miss Brill prepared to listen.

120 "No, not now," said the girl. "Not here, I can't."

"But why? Because of that stupid old thing at the end there?" asked the boy. "Why does she come here at all—who wants her? Why doesn't she keep her silly old mug[29] at home?"

"It's her fu-fur which is so funny," giggled the girl. "It's exactly like a fried
125 whiting."[30]

"Ah, be off with you!" said the boy in an angry whisper. Then: "Tell me, ma petite chérie—"[31]

"No, not here," said the girl. "Not *yet*."

On her way home she usually bought a slice of honey-cake at the baker's. It
130 was her Sunday treat. Sometimes there was an almond[32] in her slice, sometimes not. It made a great difference. If there was an almond it was like carrying home

[25]**made such a point of**: insisted on
[26]**invalid**: a sickly person
[27]**pinched**: narrow
[28]**yacht**: a small sailing ship, a cruise boat
[29]**mug**: an ugly face (slang)
[30]**whiting**: a kind of fish
[31]**ma petite chérie**: my little darling (French)
[32]**almond**: a type of small nut

a tiny present—a surprise—something that might very well not have been there. She hurried on the almond Sundays and struck the match for the kettle[33] in quite a dashing way.

135   But to-day she passed the baker's by, climbed the stairs, went into the little dark room—her room like a cupboard—and sat down on the red eiderdown. She sat there for a long time. The box that the fur came out of was on the bed. She unclasped the necklet quickly; quickly, without looking, laid it inside. But when she put the lid on she thought she heard something crying.

[33]**struck the match for the kettle**: lit her stove to boil water for tea

B. First Reading

1. Thinking about the Story

Did you feel the sadness that lay beneath the story, even when Miss Brill seemed at her happiest? Were you moved by the ending? Why?

2. Understanding the Plot

1. In what season does the story take place? How do you know?

2. What is unusual about the way Miss Brill regards her fur?

3. How long has it been since Miss Brill last wore her fur?

4. What is special about the band that Sunday afternoon?

5. Why is Miss Brill disappointed in the old man and woman who are sharing the bench? With whom does she compare them?

6. What word would you use to describe what the gentleman in gray does to the woman in the ermine toque?

7. With what does Miss Brill compare the Sunday afternoon scenes she witnesses? How does she see herself? How does she initially see the young couple?

8. How often does Miss Brill go to the park?

9. How does she earn her living?

10. What is different for Miss Brill about this Sunday afternoon's return from the park?

11. What is Miss Brill's financial situation? Give details to support your answer.

C. Second Reading

1. Exploring Themes

You are now ready to reread "Miss Brill." Note how Katherine Mansfield unfolds in painstaking detail the scenes that Miss Brill witnesses until everything is as vivid as it would be in a movie, a play, or a complex painting. Be sensitive to the gently sad atmosphere that pervades the story.

1. What role does the season play in the story?

2. What does the fur symbolize in the story? Be as detailed as possible in your answer.

3. What does the thrill Miss Brill gets from eavesdropping (listening in on other people's conversations) tell us about the kind of life she leads?

4. What is ironic about the way Miss Brill sees the silent old people who frequent the park? (lines 50–54)
Note: For information on irony.

5. What later scene does the incident with the "ermine toque" foreshadow? (lines 64–78) Explain the parallels.

6. Discuss the implications of the ending.

2. Analyzing the Author's Style

For more information on the literary terms in this section, see the explanations of *synecdoche* and *simile* below.

Synecdoche

Katherine Mansfield makes interesting use of **synecdoche**, a figure of speech in which a part is used to describe a whole. For example, Miss Brill refers to the woman she sees and pities as *an ermine toque.* (line 64) In this example, the woman's fur hat both represents her person and also draws attention to the symbolic parallels between her fur hat and Miss Brill's fur wrap.

With a partner, decide what the following sentences mean. Point out the synecdoche in each sentence, and explain the whole that the part stands for. Then see what other examples of synecdoche you can think of.

1. The rancher who owns 50,000 head of cattle was arrested last week.

2. Their brother had the reputation of being the heart and soul of any party he attended.

3. Since I have to earn my bread, I cannot afford to take a long vacation.

4. The orchestra's strong point is its strings.

5. Our neighbor recently won an important award for his rhyme.

6. Let me introduce you to the brains behind this project.

7. The captain yelled for all hands on deck during the storm.

8. In spite of all our misfortunes, we still have a roof over our head.

Simile

"Miss Brill" resonates with **similes** (explicit comparisons that use *like* or *as* to unite the two elements). For example, the story opens with a description of a blue sky with *great spots of light like white wine.* (line 1) Here, the two elements compared are light and wine, and the effect is an image of crisp, sparkling afternoon light.

1. What other simile can be found in the first paragraph? What two elements are being compared?

2. As Miss Brill observes the passing parade, she often registers what the people are doing in terms of similes. How many such similes can you find? Name them. How do these similes add color to the descriptions?

3. What does the young girl compare Miss Brill's fur to? What does this simile suggest about the appearance of the fur? How does it contradict Miss Brill's own image of her fur?

4. What simile is used to describe Miss Brill's room? What is the full effect of using this simile?

3. Judging for Yourself

Express yourself as personally as you like in your answers to the following questions.

1. Do you think Miss Brill will return to the park on the following Sunday? Justify your answer.

2. In your view, was Miss Brill wrong to eavesdrop? Should eavesdroppers always be prepared to hear something hurtful about themselves?

3. Do you feel that Miss Brill will ever take her fur out of the box again? Explain your answer.

4. What do you imagine a regular weekday to be like for Miss Brill?

5. Did you sympathize with Miss Brill's need for fantasy?

4. Making Connections

Discuss the following questions with a partner.

1. Who are the loneliest segments of the population in your country? Explain why they are so lonely.

2. What facilities are there in your hometown for people to get together and socialize? Have you made use of any of these facilities?

3. Is there a correlation between age, gender, and poverty in your country?

4. Have you ever witnessed anybody being humiliated or been in that situation your-self? Describe what happened.

5. Debate

Debate this proposition:

Lonely people have only themselves to blame.

D. FOCUS ON LANGUAGE

1. Verbs of Movement

Katherine Mansfield employs a variety of verbs to describe the leg, arm, and hand movements of her characters.

Look at the following list of verbs taken from the text, although not necessarily in the same form or tense.

stroke (line 15)	dab (line 67)
flap (line 24)	flick (line 73)
clasp (line 29)	patter (line 78)
parade (line 44)	hobble (line 81)
stagger (line 48)	trot (line 85)

Make two columns—one for leg movements and one for hand/arm movements—and list each word in the appropriate column. Then complete the paragraph that follows with the appropriate verbs. Make sure you use the correct form and tense of each verb.

Miss Brill _____ her forehead with her handkerchief as she sat watching the scene unfold in front of her. As the people _____ before her in twos and threes, she _____ her fur absentmindedly. She felt sorry for the old man who came _____ forward, _____ his cane tightly. She watched as a puppy _____ up to the playing children and wagged its tail. An anxious mother rushed up, _____ her arms wildly to shoo it away, but the puppy, unafraid, went on lightly _____ after them. Miss Brill smiled when a toddler began _____ uncertainly toward her, then gasped as she witnessed the man in gray _____ the cigarette ash off his jacket while he brutally turned his back on the woman in the ermine toque.

2. Building Vocabulary Skills

Look at the following adjectives from the story.

embroidered (line 30)
slender (line 55)
drooping (line 55)
dignified (line 65)
queer (line 93)

frail (line 97)
resolute (line 110)
trembling (line 119)
dashing (line 134)

With the help of your dictionary, find a synonym for each adjective. Then write sentences using each adjective in a context that illustrates its meaning.

E. WRITING ACTIVITIES

1. Write an essay of two to three pages examining the situation of older single women in your culture. Begin your essay with this statement: *In general, my culture extends/ does not extend the same respect to an older single woman as it gives to an older married woman.* Go on to explain the reasons and show the economic and social consequences. Conclude your essay with a comment on whether the present situation is likely to change and why.

2. Select a place where you can watch a parade of people. Note carefully what they are doing, saying, and wearing. Then, using the lively pictorial writing in lines 28–82 of "Miss Brill" as a model, write three paragraphs on what you have observed. Try to include original similes in your piece.

3. The aging single woman is frequently treated as a lonely, tragic figure in literature, epitomized by the fading beauty Blanche DuBois in Tennessee Williams's play *A Streetcar Named Desire*. Write an essay of one to two pages about a play, book, or movie you are familiar with in which an older unmarried woman plays a central role. Briefly describe her role and say whether the woman is presented in a positive or negative light.

Reading for Vocabulary

A. GETTING STARTED

Discuss the questions with your classmates.

- *How many people are there in your family? Is this a good number? Why or why not?*
- *What is the average family size in your country? Is there a trend toward having larger or smaller families?*
- *What are the advantages and disadvantages of larger and smaller families?*

B. ASSESSING YOUR VOCABULARY KNOWLEDGE: TARGET WORDS

Look at the words in the box. These are the target words for this chapter. Use the scale to score yourself on each word. After you finish the chapter, score yourself again to check your improvement.

1. I don't know this word.

2. I have seen or heard this word before, but I am not sure of the meaning.

3. I understand this word when I see it or hear it in a sentence, but I don't know how to use it in my own speaking and writing.

4. I know this word and can use it in my own speaking and writing.

TARGET WORD			
_____ assistance	_____ cooperate	_____ maintain	_____ purchase
_____ available	_____ domestic	_____ minority	_____ rely
_____ consist	_____ function	_____ negative	_____ resource
_____ consume	_____ isolation	_____ network	_____ structure
_____ contribute	_____ labor	_____ nuclear	_____ transition
_____ conversely	_____ locate	_____ promote	_____ trend

C. READING

*This passage is adapted from an introductory textbook on sociology. The passage focuses on a typical model of the family and how it is changing. As you read, pay special attention to the target vocabulary words in **bold**.*

FAMILY STRUCTURE

1   Although the **function**, or purpose, of families around the world is similar, family **structure** differs significantly from society to society and even from group to group. Because family **structure** is such an important aspect of pre-modern and modern societies, it has always been a special focus in the social sciences.

Kinship vs. Family

2   Sociologists and anthropologists make an important distinction between the family and the kinship group, although both are commonly called "families" in English. *Kinship* refers to a social **network** of people who are related by common ancestry or origin, by marriage, or by adoption. Kin can include close relatives such as parents, and distant relatives such as third cousins. Kin do not always live together or **function** as a group, but they may recognize certain rights, responsibilities, and obligations to one another. For example, in American society, kin may come together for Thanksgiving or a family reunion.

3   In contrast, a *family* is a relatively small **domestic** group that *does* **function** as a **cooperative** unit. In the United States, the family is usually a group **consisting** of parents and their children. In many societies, though, the family includes relatives from three or more generations. For example, a group of brothers and their wives, their sons and their unmarried daughters, and their sons' wives and children may live together or near one another, **cooperating** to raise food, **maintain** the home, and care for children and the elderly. If the individuals **function** as a single unit, sociologists consider them to be a family. If, however, they simply live next door to one another and do not pool their **resources**, they are viewed as separate families even though they may be related.

4   During their lifetimes, most people are members of two different types of family groups: the family into which they were born and the family that they create when they marry and have children. Societies differ in the cultural emphasis they place on these two groups. Among the Pueblo Indians, for example, the family a person is born into is given a special significance, whereas the family a person marries into is treated more casually. When a Pueblo Indian couple marry, the woman stays in her mother's household, and her husband moves in. If the couple do not get along and divorce, the husband moves back to his mother's household with little fuss.

Nuclear and Extended Families

5   Although the culturally ideal Western family is the **nuclear** family—a two-generation family group that **consists** of a father and mother and their children, usually living apart from other relatives—variations on this pattern are common. Death and divorce can leave households with only one parent. An elderly grandparent may join the household. Economic problems may force a married child to bring his or her spouse and children to live with the family. When a family is a group that **consists** of three or more generations, it is called an *extended family*.

6   The two-parent **nuclear** family is most typical of the middle and upper classes, and while the single-parent family is found in all social classes, it is more common among the lower classes. Single-parent families are generally the result of divorce and separation, out-of-wedlock birth, and male unemployment. The extended family is also more common among the lower classes, mainly because of economic conditions.

A nuclear family

7   Most middle-class **nuclear** families can afford to hire someone to babysit for their children, to help them move to a new house, or to care for the sick. They are able to borrow money from the bank when they need it for emergencies or for luxury items, such as a new car. Thus there are few economic reasons for a middle-class family to be extended.

8   The **purchase** of certain products and services is a luxury that poorer families often cannot afford. Such families generally must **rely** on family members and relatives to provide the goods and services they cannot afford to buy. A cousin will babysit. A brother will lend money to his sister until the next payday. A grandmother will take the children to a doctor if necessary. Without this **network** of shared **assistance**, families with low incomes would not be able to provide for their needs or handle many types of emergencies. The more family members who are **available**, the more likely each one is to get **assistance**. Thus, large extended families with strong ties can be a real advantage—indeed, a necessity—for lower-income families.

An extended family

The Global Trend Toward Nuclear Families

9   Family **structure** around the world has been gradually changing in the direction of the **nuclear** family. This **transition** is thought to have begun in pre-industrial rural England; at that time and place, families of three or more generations were already a distinct **minority**.

10   Today, the **trend** toward the **nuclear** family seems to be closely associated with the urbanization, industrialization, and modernization of societies. As industry replaces agriculture as the main form of work, younger family members typically leave the farms and rural villages and move to the cities where jobs are **located**, often weakening ties with those left behind. Once in the cities, families continue to move for employment and other reasons (such as better housing conditions, retirement, and more comfortable weather). The agricultural family is likely to be extended and tied to a piece of land, while the industrial family is **nuclear** and much more mobile.

11   The decline of the extended family is thus **promoted** by the changing nature of work. In rural societies, as among the poor in industrial societies, the extended family offers an economic advantage. Each member of the family does some productive work. Less able-bodied family members, such as children, the elderly, or members

with a disability, can each **contribute** in some way to the economic interests of the family unit. In industrial societies, **conversely**, these family members are treated as less essential economically and are employed only under certain conditions (for example, when there is a **labor** shortage). They therefore produce little for the family unit, yet they **consume** at about the same rate as do producers. The extended family can therefore be a disadvantage in industrial societies.

12   The **transition** from the extended to the **nuclear** family has brought with it much greater freedom and personal mobility for the individual. In the extended family, an individual's needs are generally of lesser importance compared to the demands of the larger group. Privacy, for example, is hard to find. However, there are **negative** features to the **nuclear** family, too. Although individuals are freed from a wide variety of responsibilities and obligations, other family members are no longer as responsible for them. Because the family is now a smaller unit, emotional and economic support may be more limited as each family member has fewer people **available** to turn to for companionship or **assistance**. The result may be the increased social **isolation** of individuals.

Adapted from Popenoe, D. (1995). *Sociology*, 10th ed. Englewood Cliffs, NJ: Prentice Hall, pp. 310–313.

1. Reading Comprehension

Respond to the questions in writing. Base your responses on the reading and your own personal experiences.

1. What is the difference between a family and a kinship group?

2. In what ways do economic factors, such as income level and employment, affect family structure?

3. This reading was published in 1995. What new trends in family structure have you observed in the twenty-first century? Describe how the family is changing.

2. Reading Strategy: Identifying Extended Definitions

Common words can take on specific meanings when used in a particular discipline. For example, in economics, the word *supply* means the amount of a product that a producer is willing and able to sell at a specified price; *demand* is the amount of a product a buyer is willing and able to buy at a specified price.

In other cases, a word or concept may be so complex that it cannot be easily defined in a sentence or two—for example, *culture* or *poverty*. In both of these cases, authors write extended definitions. These may vary in length from a single paragraph, to an essay, to an entire book.

An extended definition includes three of the main elements of a formal definition—the term, the word class, and the specific details for the term. But the author goes beyond these and develops the definition using one or more of the following methods: analysis, comparison/contrast, description, exemplification, etymology (word origin), or cause/effect.

The reading "Family Structure" is an extended definition of the concept of family. Review the reading and then complete the outline of how the author has developed this definition.

1. Introduction (Paragraph 1)

Section 1, Comparison and Contrast of Two Similar Terms: Kinship Vs. Family

2. Definition of *kinship*:

| Kinship | is | | who | | . |

Examples of kin: _____

3. Definition of *family*:

| Family | is | | that | | . |

Examples of family members: _____

	Kinship	**Family**
Comparison:	*a group of people*	
Contrast:		

4. Two types of families:

| | and | |

Section 2, Two Further Types of Family Groups: Nuclear and Extended Families

5. Definition of *nuclear family*:

| A nuclear family | is | | that | | . |

Definition of *extended family*:

| An extended family | is | | that | | . |

6. Relationship between class and family type:

upper classes	→	
middle classes	→	*two-parent and single-parent nuclear families*
lower classes	→	

7. and 8. Causes and effects of class on family type:

Causes   **Effects**

| 1. *income sufficient to pay for goods and services* |
| 2. |

→

| |

| 1. |
| 2. |

→

| *extended family* |

Section 3, Causes and Effects of Changes in Family Structure: The Global Trend Toward Nuclear Families

9. When family structure began to change:

| |

Type of change:

| |

10. Reasons for changes:

	and		and	*urbanization*
The agricultural family is			and	.
The industrial family is	*more mobile*		and	.

11. Pros and cons of extended families:

Pros   **Cons**

	and	*In urban families, extra family members are costly because they produce little or nothing.*

12. Pros and cons of nuclear families:

Pros   **Cons**

	and	

D. FOCUSING ON VOCABULARY

1. Word Meaning

When you encounter an unfamiliar word, remember to look for context clues to determine the word's meaning. Look at the example. Suppose that you came across the word **isolation**, but did not know the exact meaning of the word.

Example:

People living in **isolation** are often lonely.
(*You know that lonely people are often by themselves, or apart from other people.*)

People with dangerous diseases are often held in **isolation** areas in hospitals so that other people do not catch their disease.
(*You know that people with dangerous diseases must often be kept away from other people so that their disease will not spread.*)

From the context of each sentence, you can determine that *isolation* means "the state or act of being apart from others."

A. *Read the sentences and choose the word or phrase that best matches the meaning of the target word. Use context clues to determine the correct meaning. Check your dictionary if you are not sure of the answer. The first one has been done for you.*

1. Jobs requiring unskilled **labor** are often more physical than those requiring skilled **labor**, as can be seen when comparing the job of a farmhand with that of a computer operator.

   a. process

   b. employment

   c. workers

2. Exercise and sensible eating are necessary to **maintain** a healthy body.

   a. increase

   b. destroy

   c. keep up

3. Italians are a small ethnic **minority** in Canada.

   a. larger part of a big group

   b. a small part of a larger group

   c. exactly 50 percent of a group

4. Anger and hate are **negative** emotions.

   a. bad or harmful

   b. good or helpful

   c. somewhat good or helpful

5. Some supporters of democracy have tried to **promote** its development worldwide.

   a. encourage

   b. advertise

   c. diminish

6. Gold and diamonds are two of South Africa's most valuable natural **resources**.

   a. possessions with little value

   b. possessions with no value

   c. useful possessions

7. The **structure** of an English sentence includes a subject, verb, and object, or complement.

   a. element

   b. arrangement or organization

   c. process

8. The **transition** between high school and college can be difficult, which is why many students drop out.

   a. skill or ability

   b. confusion

   c. act or process of changing

9. At the beginning of the twenty-first century, most stock markets were in a downward **trend**.

   a. situation without change

   b. confused situation

   c. general way things are changing

10. Some Pueblo cliff dwellings are **located** in Mesa Verde National Park, Colorado.

    a. in a particular place

    b. convenient

    c. established

11. Janet is Steve's wife. **Conversely**, Steve is Janet's husband.

    a. in speaking of this

    b. because of this

    c. in an opposite way

B. *Read the sentences and use context to figure out the meaning of the target words. Look for a core meaning that provides a general understanding of each target word. Write the meaning in your own words. The first one has been done for you.*

1. a. People often **assist** the police by describing what happened during a crime.
   b. The rescue service provided **assistance** to the ship in trouble.

   assist *help or support* _____

2. a. Before you write a check, you must be sure that you have enough money **available** in the bank to cover the amount.
   b. The government wished to increase the **availability** of affordable health care to poorer people.

   available _____

3. a. A month **consists** of twenty-eight to thirty-one days.
   b. A square is a shape **consisting** of four equal sides and four 90-degree angles.

   consist _____

4. a. Doctors recommend that people **consume** two liters of water (about eight glasses) daily.
   b. Car manufacturers are now able to lower fuel **consumption** because technological advances have made engines more efficient.

   consume _____

5. a. **Cooperation** between teachers and parents can do much to improve a child's education.
   b. Conversation analysts have found that women tend to be **cooperative** in conversations, while men tend to be competitive.

   cooperate _____

6. a. Those who are unable to **contribute** money to the school building fund may help by giving their time.
   b. Employees may **contribute** a percentage of their monthly salary to a pension fund, which will be paid back to them after age 65 or at the time of retirement.

   contribute _____

7. a. The police were called to the family's home to settle a **domestic** argument.
   b. The artist painted a scene of happy **domesticity**—a large family sitting around the table eating a festive meal.

   domestic _____

8. a. The **function** of the telephone is to provide easy, convenient communication.
   b. Even though the factory was a century old, all of the equipment was still **functional** and worked perfectly.

   function _____

9. a. The Paris Metro—one of the best subway systems in the world—consists of a vast **network** of interconnected train lines.
   b. The interlibrary loan **network** enables students and staff to borrow library books from other universities in the state.

   network _____

10. a. Many students prefer to rent formal clothing for dances and balls because the cost of **purchasing** such items is so high.
    b. The family used most of its money for the **purchase** of food and clothing.

    purchase _____

11. a. These days, many families **rely** on both the husband and wife working in order to earn enough money for daily living.
    b. Bus use in the city is low because most commuters feel they cannot **rely** on a service that is regularly late.

    rely _____

> **Word Tip**
> Paragraph 5 of "Family Structure" defines the phrase **_nuclear family_** as "a two-generation family group that consists of a father and mother and their children, usually living apart from other relatives." This is a unique use of the term **_nuclear_** that only applies for the collocation **_nuclear family._** All other uses of the word **_nuclear_** refer to the central part of an atom and its uses in atomic energy or warfare.

2. Word Families

When using new words in writing, learners often select a word with the right meaning, but the wrong word form, or part of speech. Checking your writing to ensure that you have used the correct form is a very important step in editing your work.

You should choose the word form based on the function each word performs in your sentences. Does the word stand for a person, place, thing, or event (noun), does it describe a noun (adjective), is it an action or a state (verb), or does it describe an action (adverb)? Different word forms may have different spellings. If you do not know the correct spelling of a word form, use your dictionary to help you.

Read the sentences. In six of the sentences, an incorrect form of the target word has been used. If the form of the target word is incorrect, cross it out and write the correct form. If the form is correct, put a checkmark (✓). The first two have been done for you.

1. ___*availability*___ The building boom in the city has increased the **available** of cheap office space.

2. _____✓_____ The **transitional** government carried out the work of the nation until the elections were held six months later.

3. _____ Automobile associations believe that new roads must be built to solve traffic problems. **Converse**, environmentalists believe that new roads simply add to these problems.

4. _____ Products that are sold for both **domestic** and restaurant use are sometimes packaged differently.

5. _____ **Isolating** is one form of punishment that prisons use for difficult criminals.

6. _____ After the storm, there was only one **functioning** telephone in the area.

7. _____ Fifteen percent of the world's people **consuming** sixty-eight percent of the world's energy.

8. _____ One objective of education in any country is the **promotion** of that country's cultural values.

9. _____ Like the family, the workplace can only operate if there is a clear **structurally**.

10. _____ An individual's daily **contributor** to the world's pollution problems may seem small, but when added together over years, it is significant.

3. Collocation

Fluent users of a language have become used to the natural patterns in which words appear. As a language learner, it will be easier for others to understand you if you use these same natural patterns. A number of the words in this unit form word partnerships, or collocations. This means that when one word occurs in the pair, it naturally suggests the word or words around it. Remember that collocations often fall into simple patterns.

Example:

noun + verb   verb + noun   noun + noun

adjective + noun   verb + adverb

Match each target word in the box with the group of words that regularly occur with it. If the (~) symbol appears before a word in a list (e.g., ~shortage), the target word comes before the word in the list (e.g., **labor** shortage). In all other cases, the target word comes after the word in the list, as in unskilled **labor.** The first one has been done for you.

consist	~~labor~~	minority	resources
consumer	location	network	trend

1. _____labor_____

~shortage

~saving

~market

unskilled

2. _____

sizeable

ethnic

~groups

~communities

3. _____

~primarily of

~exclusively of

~largely of

~essentially of

4. _____

decide on a

ideal

pinpoint a

perfect

5. _____

~rights

~confidence

~goods

~protection

6. _____

reverse a

downward

follow a

observe a

7. _____

allocate

build up

waste

exhaust

8. _____

old boy

extensive

computer

nationwide

E. EXPANDING THE TOPIC

1. *Read the statements about family life in the chart. Evaluate each statement. Is it an advantage of living in a* **nuclear** *family or an extended family? Place a checkmark (✓) in the appropriate box. If the factor is equally advantageous for both types of family structure, check the "equal advantage" box. Then discuss your opinions with a partner.*

Statements	Advantage of Living in a Nuclear Family	Advantage of Living in an Extended Family	Equal Advantage for Both Family Types
1. There are more people working, helping to **maintain** a steady income during economic slowdowns.			
2. Parents **rely** on their children to help with housework.			
3. There are fewer people who will ask for your **assistance**.			
4. There are more people around, so there is less chance of feeling lonely and **isolated**.			
5. Family members that **cooperate** with one another can do things that they could not do by themselves.			
6. **Domestic** decision making requires less discussion.			
7. Working family members contribute to the family's **purchasing** power.			
8. Expectations of relatives can have a **negative** impact on a couple's freedom.			

2. Your Turn

Write an essay about one of the topics. Be sure to support your ideas with clear examples.

- *How has family size changed in your home country since you were a child? Explain why these changes have occurred.*
- *What effects do changes in family size have on women? Explain. What effects do changes in family size have on children? Explain.*

Appendix 1

Speed Reading

A. GUIDELINES FOR TIMED READING PRACTICE

- *Be sure to record the exact time you start and finish each passage.*
- *Answer the questions without looking back at the passages.*
- *Check your answers with your teacher. Then look back at the text to understand any incorrect answers.*
- *Find your reading rate on the Reading Rate Table on page 75.*
- *After you have read both passages, check your progress on the charts for reading rate and comprehension. Your aim should be to increase your reading rate gradually while keeping your comprehension score at 75 percent or more.*
  - *If your reading rate stays the same, you need to force your eyes to move ahead faster.*
  - *If you have incorrect answers for more than three questions, you might be reading too fast. Slow down slightly and concentrate more while you read.*

Above material from: *Advanced Reading Power 4*

B. KEEPING TRACK OF YOUR READING RATE 1

Looking back on a decade of cultural growth, last week's tenth annual University of California at Irvine [UCI] Rainbow Festival and Conference focused on "Reflecting on Our Faces and Dreams." "Rainbow Festival was created 10 years ago [in 1984] as a means to provide educational forums to increase the awareness of cultural diversity," said Corina Espinoza, chair of the conference. This year's festival featured workshops, seminars and speakers addressing the issues of diversity and multiculturalism. Ring Road of the UCI Student Center served as the location for displaying ethnic arts and crafts, performances by student clubs and organizations, and a variety of foods from different cultures.

Opening the two-day conference period was keynote speaker Audrey Yamagata-Noji, dean of student development at Rancho Santiago College in Santa Ana. She spoke on the theme of the festival at the Cross Cultural Center and on "recognizing the faces around us and realizing that all those faces have dreams," Espinoza said. The evening keynote speaker was Gregory Alan-Williams, Emmy award-winning actor and author of the book "Gathering Heroes: Reflections on Rage and Responsibility." He did not advocate diversity as being something new but "as American as apple pie."

Maceo Hernandez, referred to as the "Demon Drummer from East L.A.," along with John Esaki, put on a Japanese taiko drum presentation. . . . "You'd think that drumming with him would be intimidating, but taiko brings everybody together. You can bond with taiko," said Peggy Kamon, a senior English major. "It was kind of a thrill," added Miki Takushi. . . .

According to Espinoza, the planning committee for this year tried to schedule more events so that more people could attend at different times of the day. Three evening sessions of a workshop entitled "Walk in My Shoes" explored different cultural backgrounds and trying to be more sensitive to the way others feel. The session was located in the student dormitories. They also provided various afternoon performances at the cultural fair in the Ring Road so people could attend during the lunch hour.

In order to reach out to the surrounding community, a new evening cultural performance, "A Musical Mosaic," was presented in Crystal Cove Auditorium. This final performance featured the song and dance of different ethnic and cultural traditions, including the American Indian "Fancy Shawl" dance, the Hawaiian chants and hula of Na Opio Ka'aina, the songs of the Royal Scottish Country Dance Society, and the Filipino dance by Kababayan.

Starting Time _____

(400 Words)   **Finishing Time** _____

Reading Time _____

Story by Meghan Sweeney, reprinted from *New University Newspaper*, November 7, 1994.

A. Now mark these statements true **(T)** *or false* **(F)** *without looking back at the reading.*

1. _____ This event took place at a high school campus.

2. _____ UCI students come from many cultural backgrounds.

3. _____ This was the tenth Rainbow Festival at UCI.

4. _____ All of the festival events took place in the evening.

5. _____ Hernandez and Esaki, two musicians from different cultures, performed together.

6. _____ Only groups representing countries outside of the United States performed at the festival.

7. _____ The festival included workshops, dancing, and music, but not food.

8. _____ Students who were interviewed seemed to enjoy the conference and festival.

9. _____ The school administration probably supports the need for cultural understanding among groups.

10. _____ This festival is probably called Rainbow Festival because it is held on a bright sunny day.

Percent correct = _____   **Words per minute (wpm) =** _____

C. Reading Rate Table 1

Reading Time (minutes: seconds)	Rate (words per minute)	Reading Time (minutes: seconds)	Rate (words per minute)
:30 sec	800 wpm		
:35	686	2:10	185
:40	597	2:15	178
:45	533	2:20	172
:50	480	2:25	166
:55	440	2:30	160
1:00	400	2:35	155
1:05	370	2:40	149
1:10	345	2:45	145
1:15	320	2:50	141
1:20	300	2:55	137
1:25	282	3:00	133
1:30	267	3:15	123
1:35	253	3:30	114
1:40	240	3:45	107
1:45	229	4:00	100
1:50	219	4:15	94
1:55	209	4:30	89
2:00	200	4:45	84
2:05	192	5:00	80

Example:

A. *Write your exact starting time. Preview the passage for a few seconds and then read it all the way through to the end. Push yourself to read a little faster than usual.*

Starting time _____
(Write the exact time
you begin reading.)

D. Keeping Track of Your Reading Rate 2

Using Cell Phones: Cultural Differences

What do you do if your cell phone rings while you are with a group of people? If you are French, you will probably ignore the call. If you are English, you may walk away from the group to answer it. If you are Spanish, you are likely to answer it there in the middle of the group and invite everyone around you to join the conversation.

As many travelers have noticed, there are considerable differences from one country to another in the way people use their cell phones. This has been confirmed by a recent study of cell phone use in three European cities—Madrid, London, and Paris. In spite of the fact that these cities are all in the European Union and share a great deal of history and culture, local customs are still very different. These customs influence the way people in these cities use their phones in public.

According to Amparo Lasén, the Spanish sociologist who conducted the study, there were no real surprises for anyone who is familiar with the customs in these cities. Lasén interviewed people and observed their behavior in three different settings: a major train station, a commercial area, and a business district in each city.

She found that Londoners use their cell phones the least in public. If they are with others, they prefer to let calls be answered by voice mail (a recorded message) and then they check for messages later. If the English do answer a call on the street, they seem to dislike talking with others around. They tend to move away from a crowded sidewalk and seek out a place where they cannot be heard, such as the far side of a subway entrance or even the edge of a street. They seem to feel that the danger of the traffic is preferable to the risk of having their conversation be overheard.

This has led to a behavior that Lasén has called "clustering." At a busy time of day on the streets of London, you may find small crowds of cell phone users grouped together, each one talking into a cell phone. Even when it is raining—as it often is in London—people still prefer not to hold their conversations where others could hear. They talk under their umbrellas or in a doorway.

In Madrid, on the other hand, few people use voice mail because the Spanish dislike talking with machines rather than real voices. If there is no answer, they don't leave a message. They prefer to try again later or wait for a return call. And since the Spanish are not shy about answering their calls in public, the call may come sooner than it would in London or Paris. In fact, in Madrid it is common to hear loud and lively phone conversations on the street, accompanied by shouts, laughter and the waving of hands. In fact, sometimes it happens that a group of friends may be walking down the street together, each talking on their own phone, but smiling and nodding as though it were one large conversation that everyone could hear.

Even when they are not using their phones, the Spanish often hold them in their hands as they walk down the street or put them on the table at a restaurant, so they will not miss any incoming calls. In a movie theater, not only do cell phones occasionally ring, but people sometimes answer them and have brief conversations.

In Paris, however, there are stricter rules about how and when to use cell phones. It is not considered polite to use a phone in a restaurant, for instance, though it might be acceptable in the more informal setting of a café. One special custom that has developed in cafés seems unique to Paris. Young women often place their cell phones on the table beside them to signal that they are expecting someone. When the friend arrives, the phone is put away. In fact, the French are generally very disapproving of phone use in public and are quick to express that disapproval, even to strangers.

In one area, sociologists found that the French and Spanish were similar. Both were quite willing to continue a phone conversation in a romantic situation, even kissing someone present while continuing a conversation on the phone. These people were clearly not using videophones. In London, however, no one was ever observed to be kissing while on the telephone. The English seem to prefer more privacy for their romantic moments.

According to Lasén, cultural stereotypes were supported by yet another difference that she noticed as she conducted her study. In each of the three cities, people reacted to her differently when she was interviewing and observing. In Paris, people frowned at her; in London, they pretended not to notice; in Madrid, however, they did not seem to mind.

Understanding the habits of these European cell phone users has become a lively topic of study for sociologists and psychologists at European universities. But with 1 billion cell phone users around the world, the subject is of interest not only to academic researchers. Habits of cell phone use are also a matter of serious study by telecommunications companies. If they can understand the local customs and customers better, they might be able to change people's behavior and increase cell phone use. For example, if phone companies want to increase their profits in France, they need to convince people that it is acceptable to use their phones in restaurants. The Spanish need to be persuaded that voice mail is not so bad, and the English must learn to leave their phones on all the time.

Source: Adapted from "A Mobile Tale of Three Cities" by Thomas Crampton. *International Herald Tribune*, June 11–12, 2005.

Finishing time _____
(Write the exact time that
you finish reading.)

Reading time _____
(Subtract your starting time from your
finishing time.)

B. *Write your exact finishing time (minutes and seconds) and reading time. Then answer the comprehension questions. Do not look back at the passage while you are answering the questions.*

C. *Circle the letter of the best answer for each item.*

1. Choose the statement that best expresses the thesis (general idea) of this passage.

   a. People in different cities have different social customs.

   b. Londoners do not like to use their cell phones in public.

   c. The way people use cell phones differs in London, Paris, and Madrid.

   d. People in Madrid tend to speak more loudly than in Paris or London.

2. A Spanish sociologist has said that the way people use their cell phones

   a. fits in with their local habits and customs.

   b. is the same in all European countries today.

   c. is related to the person's sex and age.

   d. depends on where they use their phone.

3. Londoners use voice mail a lot because they

   a. enjoy leaving recorded messages.

   b. like to answer calls in crowded places.

   c. do not like to speak with real voices.

   d. prefer not to answer calls in public.

4. In London, people speaking on phones "cluster" together so they can share their conversation with others.

   a. True

   b. False

5. When they are in groups, the people in Madrid

   a. prefer to pay more attention to the people around them.

   b. continue to answer calls and have phone conversations.

   c. stop talking and wait when a cell phone rings.

   d. prefer to leave messages with voice mail.

6. In Paris, a cell phone on a café table beside a young woman means she is expecting someone.

   a. True

   b. False

7. Parisians

   a. do not like it when people use cell phones in public.

   b. use cell phones more than the English or the Spanish.

   c. use their cell phones often in restaurants and movie theaters.

   d. never continue a phone conversation in a romantic moment.

8. You can infer (or conclude) from this passage that

   a. cell phone companies will make less money in the European countries.

   b. sociologists can tell little about people's lives from their phone use.

   c. weather can be an important factor in the way people use cell phones.

   d. technology may be global, but the way people use it is not.

Appendix 1   Above material from: *Advanced Reading Power 4*

E. Reading Rate Table 2

These passages are about 950 words long. To determine your reading rate in this table, find the time that is closest to your Reading Time. Then look across to find your reading rate. For instance, if you read the example passage in 2:30 (two minutes and thirty seconds) your reading rate would be 380 WPM.

Reading Time (minutes: seconds)	Rate (words per minute)	Reading Time (minutes: seconds)	Rate (words per minute)
1:00	950	3:40	260
1:10	815	3:50	248
1:20	714	4:00	238
1:30	633	4:10	228
1:40	572	4:20	219
1:50	518	4:30	211
2:00	475	4:40	204
2:10	439	4:50	197
2:20	408	5:00	190
2:30	380	5:10	184
2:40	357	5:20	178
2:50	335	5:30	173
3:00	317	5:40	168
3:10	300	5:50	163
3:20	285	6:00	158
3:30	271		

Appendix 2

Adjective Clauses

A. COMPREHENSION CHECK

Check your understanding of adjective clauses. Put a check (✓) next to the sentences that are correct.

1. _____ The company that I want to work for is small.

2. _____ The book is overdue that I borrowed from the library.

3. _____ Countries whose gun laws are strict have few gun deaths.

4. _____ Alan's father, which has a Ph.D. in chemical engineering, has high expectations for his son.

5. _____ The hero, who is in every scene of the first half of the movie, unexpectedly disappears in the second half.

6. _____ My friends recommended the restaurant that is on the corner of Irvine Avenue and Seventeenth Street.

7. _____ Countries, that have earthquakes, need strict building codes.

8. _____ Dr. Kaufman who teaches physiology will retire soon.

9. _____ The concert tickets which Carol and I bought are in my purse.

10. _____ The winter Jan worked at the ski resort was the best of her life.

B. EDITING FOCUS

Adjective clauses, also called relative clauses, are like adjectives because they identify or give more information about nouns or pronouns. Use adjective clauses to combine sentences and to make your writing more descriptive and interesting. As a writer, you must decide when adjective clauses can improve your writing and know how to construct these clauses. Compare these two examples:

- *We love the old house. It has a huge pear tree.*
- *We love the old house* **that has a huge pear tree.**

Both examples convey the same meaning, but the second example uses an adjective clause and expresses the same information in a more concise and sophisticated way.

1. Forming Adjective Clauses

1. An adjective clause is a dependent clause so it cannot stand alone. It must be connected to an independent clause to form a complex sentence. An adjective clause is introduced by a relative pronoun such as *that, who, whom, which,* and *whose.* The noun or pronoun that the relative pronoun refers to is called the antecedent.

INDEPENDENT CLAUSE   ADJECTIVE CLAUSE

Monica and Hector went to *a show* **that was four hours long**.

ANTECEDENT   RELATIVE PRONOUN

2. In most cases, the adjective clause directly follows the noun it is identifying or describing (the antecedent).

   The surprise birthday *party* **that Grant and Bob gave for Stella** was a lot of fun.
   NOT
   The surprise birthday party was a lot of fun that Grant and Bob gave for Stella.

   The man **who(m) we spoke to** gave us good advice.
   NOT
   The man gave us good advice whom we spoke to.

3. Do not use double pronouns within the adjective clause.

   Joanna's father *is the kind of person* **who never gets mad**.
   NOT
   Joanna's father is the kind of person who he never gets mad.

   This is the *program* **that Samuel and I wrote for our computer science class**.
   NOT
   This is the program that Samuel and I wrote it for our computer science class.

4. When a relative pronoun is the subject of the adjective clause, use a subject pronoun.
   - *who* or *that* for people

     Susanna baby-sits for her neighbor. Her neighbor has five children.
     Susanna baby-sits for her *neighbor* **who** has five children.

     The girls live next door. The girls are really nice.
     The *girls* **that** live next door are really nice.

   - *which* or *that* for things

     John wrote a research paper. The research paper analyzes the causes of depression.
     John wrote a *research paper* **that** analyzes the causes of depression.

     I submitted the two projects. The two projects were due today.
     I submitted the two *projects*, **which** were due today.

5. When the relative pronoun is the object of the adjective clause, use an object pronoun.
   - *whom, who,* or *that* for people

     Harry Truman governed during the late 1940s. My grandmother knew Harry Truman.
     Harry Truman, **who(m)** my grandmother knew, governed during the late 1940s.

     Appendix 2   Above material from: *Eye on Editing 2*

- *which* or *that* for things

  I bought a computer yesterday. The computer I bought will be delivered to the store tomorrow.
  The *computer* **that** I bought yesterday will be delivered to the store tomorrow.

The relative pronoun can also be the object of a preposition.

  The car **that** Rose left her purse **in** was stolen.
  The car **in which** Rose left her purse was stolen. (*formal, academic English*)

Note: When the relative pronoun is the object of the verb or object of a preposition, it can be omitted.

  The computer **that** I *bought* yesterday will be delivered tomorrow.
  The computer I bought yesterday will be delivered tomorrow.

  The car **that** Rose left her purse *in* was stolen.
  The car Rose left her purse in was stolen.

6. When a relative pronoun replaces a possessive word, use *whose* + noun.

  My sister's son just went away to college. My sister feels lonely.
  My sister, **whose son** just went away to college, feels lonely.

  The company's headquarters are in Boston. The company has offices overseas.
  The company, **whose headquarters** are in Boston, has offices overseas.

> **Tip**
> In spoken English, *whose* and *who's* sound similar. In writing, be sure to use the contraction *who's* for *who is* and *who has* and the relative pronoun *whose* to show possession.
>
>   *Who's* going to the assembly?
>
>   Russell found the child *who's* been missing for a week.
>
>   I want to work for a company **whose** profits are growing.

7. Sentences with adjective clauses must follow all subject-verb agreement rules.
   - *The subject and verb of the independent clause must agree even if they are separated by an adjective clause.*

   The chemistry **classes** *that I took last semester* **were** very interesting.
   NOT
   The chemistry classes that I took last semester was very interesting.

   - *The verb following the relative pronoun always has the same number as the antecedent.*

   Our neighbors have a *dog* **that barks** all day long. (*singular*)

   The *boys* in my dorm **who play** water polo travel a lot with the team. (*plural*)

   - *The subject and verb within the relative clause must agree.*

                          s   v
   The *textbooks* **that she is buying** cost $250.
   NOT
   The textbooks that she are buying cost $250.

> **Tip**
> Mark the subjects and verbs in sentences that use adjective clauses. Put the letter *S* above subjects, the letter *V* above verbs, and make sure each pair agrees.

8. Restrictive adjective clauses (also called identifying or defining) do not require commas. A restrictive adjective clause supplies necessary information to identify the noun that it modifies. Restrictive adjective clauses are used more frequently than nonrestrictive adjective clauses.

    A *person* **who sells stocks and bonds** is called a stockbroker.
    (*The information in the adjective clause is necessary in order to know which person is being described.*)

    Do you know the *man* **who is at the table in the corner**?
    (*The information in the adjective clause is necessary in order to know which man is being referred to.*)

9. Nonrestrictive adjective clauses (also called nonidentifying or nondefining) require commas. A nonrestrictive clause supplies additional information, not necessary to identify the noun it modifies.

    We just read <u>One Hundred Years of Solitude</u>**, which is by Gabriel Garcia Marquez.**
    (*The additional information in the adjective clause is not necessary to identify the book.*)

    *Ten Downing Street***, where the prime minister of England lives,** is a plain-looking house.
    (*The additional information in the adjective clause is not necessary to identify the address.*)

Note: Do not use the relative pronoun *that* in a nonrestrictive adjective clause.

    Old Faithful, **which** is located in Yellowstone National Park, regularly shoots water and steam into the air.
    NOT
    Old Faithful, that is located in Yellowstone National Park, regularly shoots water and steam into the air.

10. Commas around an adjective clause can change the meaning of a sentence. Compare the meanings of the following sentences:

    The students**, who wanted to study French,** had to wait in line to register.
    (*The use of commas means that all of the students wanted to study French, and all of them had to wait in line.*)

    The students **who wanted to study French** had to wait in line to register. The students who wanted to study German didn't have to wait in line.
    (*The lack of commas means that only some of the students wanted to study French. The adjective clause identifies which students had to wait in line.*)

Note: Adjective clauses can be used to describe indefinite pronouns such as *someone, anyone, everything,* and *other.*

    Someone **who wanted to speak with you** called but didn't leave a message.
    I don't know *anyone* **who has a truck**.

    Appendix 2 Above material from: *Eye on Editing 2*

2. Using Adjective Clauses

1. Use adjective clauses to combine ideas and make your sentences less short and repetitive.

   My friend is a medical student. She hopes to specialize in pediatrics.
   My friend, **who is a medical student,** hopes to specialize in pediatrics.

2. Use adjective clauses to make general sentences more specific or descriptive.

   General   They just finished a research project.
   Descriptive They just finished a research project **that analyzes the effectiveness of grammar instruction in reading classes**.

3. The relative adverbs *where* and *when* can be used to introduce adjective clauses of place and time.

   We went to *Yellowstone*, **where** we saw Old Faithful.
   The *week* **when** she was in the hospital was hard on her parents.

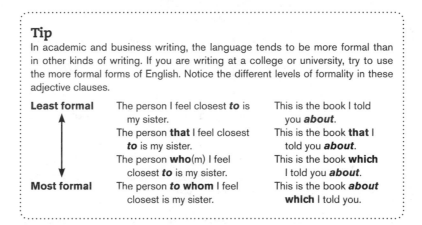

Tip

In academic and business writing, the language tends to be more formal than in other kinds of writing. If you are writing at a college or university, try to use the more formal forms of English. Notice the different levels of formality in these adjective clauses.

Least formal	The person I feel closest **to** is my sister.	This is the book I told you **about**.
	The person **that** I feel closest **to** is my sister.	This is the book **that** I told you **about**.
	The person **who**(m) I feel closest **to** is my sister.	This is the book **which** I told you **about**.
Most formal	The person **to whom** I feel closest is my sister.	This is the book **about which** I told you.

Self Check

Correct the errors in adjective clauses.

1. Professor Simms, that we had for economics, is very fair.

2. Samuel Clemens who wrote *The Adventures of Huckleberry Finn* used the pen name Mark Twain.

3. The classes Sam is taking begins next week.

4. The interview with the director of operations went very well that I had yesterday.

5. His cousins went to a wedding ceremony that it was on the beach at sunset.

C. EDITING PRACTICE

A. Put a check (✓) next to the sentences that use adjective clauses correctly. Correct the sentences that have errors.

1. _____ Thoa's father, that used to play college football, is coaching the high school team.

2. _____ The blending of cultures that we see in the United States today has both good and bad points.

3. _____ The bulbs should bloom in the spring that we planted last winter.

4. _____ The ABC software company whose president just resigned is in financial trouble.

5. _____ St. John, which is a Caribbean island, is a tropical paradise.

6. _____ The 1992 demonstration is an example of the unrest that we are going to study it in sociology.

7. _____ Extremely competitive people who always want to win damages valuable friendships.

8. _____ The woman whom the story is about lives in a small New England town.

9. _____ Galileo Galilei, whom never left Italy, was nonetheless known around the world.

10. _____ The Tasman Sea, where the poisonous box jellyfish lives, is the home of other deadly sea creatures.

11. _____ The Puerto Rican culture of the 1950s which Esmeralda Santiago writes about in *When I Was Puerto Rican* has not changed significantly in the last decades.

12. _____ Professor Williams, whose class is on Wednesday nights, is an excellent writing teacher.

B. Read the following paragraph. Complete the paragraph with the correct relative pronoun, relative adverb, or neither (Ø).

D.H. Lawrence celebrates old age in his poem *Beautiful Old Age*. Although old age is a

stage of life _____ is not always valued, Lawrence puts into words
1. when / that

some of its positive points. He says that a person _____ has led a truth-
2. who / which

ful life will live happily into old age. Old age should be a time _____
3. when / where

people feel peace from having lived a full life. Wrinkled skin, _____ is
4. that / which

inevitable, is a sign of wisdom and not of deterioration. If people believe Lawrence's words,

then maturity ought to be a stage _____ we look forward to, and the
5. who / that

elderly person _____ we fear becoming ought to be looked at as some-
6. ø / which

one _____ we strive to be. Two people _____
7. ø / where   8. whom / who

     Appendix 2   Above material from: *Eye on Editing 2*

fit this description of beautiful old age are my great grandmother and my great-aunt. Both women have lived honest lives _____ have been filled with

9. when / that

hard work and family. They are being rewarded for their work as children, grandchildren, and great grandchildren honor them daily. This is the old age that I hope to have one day—the old age that D.H. Lawrence describes and the old age _____

10. when / that

my great grandmother and great-aunt are living.

C. *In the following paragraph, five of the underlined adjective clauses are not correct. Find the errors and write the corrections above each clause.*

There are many examples today of the cultural influences (1) that powerful countries have on less powerful countries. English influence in Antigua, French influence in Vietnam, and American influence in Puerto Rico are all examples of less dominant cultures absorbing the styles and traditions of more dominant cultures. According to Jamacia Kincaid, an Antiguan writer, the gardens (2) that naturally grow in Antigua have no order to them; they are wild and natural. However, the British influence, (3) that emphasizes order and organization, can be seen in some of the gardening styles of wealthy Antiguans. Christmas trees (4) which originated in Germany have also found their way to Antigua due to British influence. In Vietnam, the French influence, (5) which was even more apparent years ago, is still obvious today. Vietnamese food and architecture, (6) which are considered traditional, have a French touch. The French language, (7) which was once the language of the educated and influential in Vietnam, still holds a position of importance. In Puerto Rico, language also plays an influential role. Spanish, (8) that is the primary language in Puerto Rico, has been replaced by English in some schools and institutions. In addition to the English language, American food and music are now part of the Puerto Rican way of life. Many Puerto Ricans can still remember the day several decades ago (9) when Americans came to their small towns to "educate" them about diet and hygiene. Many (10) whom accepted this at the time learned to resent it later. In this day and age, it is hard to stop or even to ignore worldwide influences. Cultural influence is a phenomenon (11) who's importance shouldn't go unnoticed.

D. The following paragraph has ten errors in the use of adjective clauses. Find and correct the errors.

The object that I am looking at is a three-dimensional rectangle, although sometimes this object can be the shape of a cube or a sphere. Five sides are made of glass, that is clear, and there is either a removable top or no top at all. One usually finds this object inside a house or office in a room when people are likely to meet, such as the living room, family room, or kitchen. This object is not mobile. It often has a small motor that keep the environment inside the rectangle clean. Even with this motor, the object has to be cleaned every few weeks. Plants may also be found inside of it that help keep this object clean. Next to the plants, there are sometimes figurines that they are set in brightly colored rocks. Both adults and children like this object. Some people who they have stressful lives find this object soothing and peaceful to look at. People whom have these objects usually love animals. Animals use this object for a home that live in fresh and salt water. The animals, that live in this object, make good pets for a person who he is allergic to cats and dogs. Do you know what this object is?

D. MORE PRACTICE

Read the following selection from OC Family Magazine. *Choose the correct form and use of adjective clauses.*

GET ON THE PIANO

Taking piano lessons and solving math puzzles on a computer significantly improve specific math skills of elementary schoolchildren, according to a new study.

The results, which _____ in the March issue of
      1. were published / they were published

the journal *Neurological Research*, are the latest in a series _____
      2. who / that

links musical training to the development of higher brain functions.

Researchers worked with 135 second-grade students at the 95th Street School in Los Angeles after conducting a pilot study[1] with 102 students. Children

_____ were given four months of piano training as well as time
      3. which / that

[1]**pilot study** test that is done to see if an idea or product will be successful

      Appendix 2 Above material from: *Eye on Editing 2*

playing with newly designed computer software scored 27 percent higher on math and fraction tests than other children.

Piano instruction is thought to enhance the brain's "hard wiring"[2] for spatial-temporal reasoning, or the ability to visualize and transform objects in space and time, says physics professor Gordon Shaw _____ who led the study.
<u>4. , / ø</u>

At the same time, the computer game allows children to solve geometric and math puzzles that _____ their ability to manipulate shapes in their mind.
<u>5. boosts / boost</u>

The findings are significant because a grasp of proportional math and fractions is a prerequisite to math at higher levels, and children who _____
<u>6. do not / does not</u>
master these areas of math cannot understand more advanced math that _____ critical[3] to high-tech fields.
<u>7. It is / is</u>

Students _____ used the software and played the piano also
<u>8. whom / who</u>
demonstrated a heightened ability to think ahead, Shaw says. "They were able to leap ahead several steps on problems in their heads."

Researchers plan to expand the study to six schools this fall to demonstrate its effectiveness in a variety of settings.

[2]**hard wiring** something that is not easily changed
[3]**critical** very important

Appendix 3

Connecting Words and Transition Signals

A. COORDINATING WORDS

1. Coordinating Conjunctions

Coordinating conjunctions connect grammatically equal elements. Coordinating conjunctions are sometimes called the "Fan Boys" conjunctions—For, And, Nor, But, Or, Yet, So.

Conjunction	Function	Example
for	Connects a reason to a result	I am a little hungry, **for** I didn't eat breakfast this morning.
and	Connects equal similar ideas	John likes to fish **and** hunt.
nor	Connects two negative sentences	She does not eat meat, **nor** does she drink milk.
but	Connects equal different ideas	I like to eat fish **but** not to catch them.
or	Connects two equal choices	Do you prefer coffee **or** tea?
yet	Connects equal contrasting ideas	It is sunny **yet** cold.
so	Connects a result to a reason	I did not eat breakfast this morning, **so** I am a little hungry.

2. Paired (Correlative) Conjunctions

Correlative conjunctions are always in pairs. Like coordinating conjunctions, they connect grammatically equal elements.

Conjunction Pairs	Example
both . . . and	**Both** San Francisco **and** Sydney have beautiful harbors.
not only . . . but also	Japanese food is **not only** delicious to eat **but also** beautiful to look at.
either . . . or	Bring **either** a raincoat **or** an umbrella when you visit Seattle.
neither . . . nor	My grandfather could **neither** read **nor** write, but he was a very wise person.
whether . . . or	The newlyweds could not decide **whether** to live with her parents **or** to rent an apartment.

B. SUBORDINATING WORDS

A subordinating word is the first word in a dependent clause. Common subordinating words include the following.

Subordinating Conjunctions for Adverb Clauses

Time (When?)	
after	**After** we ate lunch, we decided to go shopping.
as, just as	**Just as** we left the house, it started to rain.
as long as	We waited **as long as** we could.
as soon as	**As soon as** the front door closed, I looked for my house key.
before	I thought I had put it in my coat pocket **before** we left.
since	I have not locked myself out of the house **since** I was 10 years old.
until	**Until** I was almost 12, my mother pinned the key to my coat.
when	**When** I turned 12, my mother let me keep the key in my pocket.
whenever	I usually put the key in the same place **whenever** I come home.
while	**While** I searched for the key, it rained harder and harder.

Place (Where?)	
where	I like to shop **where** prices are low.
wherever	I try to shop **wherever** there is a sale.
anywhere	You can find bargains **anywhere** you shop.
everywhere	I use my credit card **everywhere** I shop.
Manner (How?)	
as, just as	I love to get flowers(,) **as** most women do.*
as if	You look **as if** you didn't sleep at all last night.
as though	She acts **as though** she doesn't know us.
Distance (How far? How near? How close?)	
as + *adverb* + as	We will hike **as far as** we can before it turns dark.
	The child sat **as close as** she could to her mother.
	The child sat **as close** to her mother **as** she could.
Frequency (How often?)	
as often as	I call my parents **as often as** I can.
Reason (Why?)	
as	I can't take evening classes(,) **as** I work at night.*
because	I can't take evening classes **because** I work at night.
since	I can't take evening classes **since** I work at night.
Purpose (For what purpose?)	
so that	Many people emigrate **so that** their children can have a better life.
in order that	Many people emigrate **in order that** their children can have a better life.
Result (With what result?)	
so + *adjective* + that	I was **so tired** last night **that** I fell asleep at dinner.
so + *adverb* + that	She talks **so softly that** the other students cannot hear her.
such a(n) + *noun* + that	It was **such an easy test that** most of the students got A's.
so much/many/little/few + *noun* + that	He is taking **so many classes that** he has no time to sleep.

*This is an exception to the usual rule for commas. Many writers use a comma before *as*.

Condition (Under what condition?)	
if	We will not go hiking **if** it rains.
unless	We will not go hiking **unless** the weather is perfect.
Partial Contrast	
although	I love my brother **although** we disagree about almost everything.
even though	I love my brother **even though** we disagree about almost everything.
though	I love my brother **though** we disagree about almost everything.
Contrast (Direct opposites)	
while	My brother likes classical music, **while** I prefer hard rock.
whereas	He dresses conservatively, **whereas** I like to be a little shocking.

Subordinating Words for Adjective Clauses

To Refer to People	
who, whom, whose, that (informal)	People **who** live in glass houses should not throw stones.
	My parents did not approve of the man **whom** my sister married.
	An orphan is a child **whose** parents are dead.
To Refer to Animals and Things	
which	My new computer, **which** I bought yesterday, stopped working today.
that	Yesterday I received an e-mail **that** I did not understand.
To Refer to a Time or a Place	
when	Thanksgiving is a time **when** families travel great distances to be together.
where	An orphanage is a place **where** orphans live.

Appendix 3 Above material from: *Writing Academic English Level 4, Fourth Edition*

Subordinating Words for Noun Clauses

That Clauses	
that	Do you believe **that** there is life in outer space?
***If/Whether* Clauses**	
whether	I can't remember **whether** I locked the door.
whether or not	**whether or not** I locked the door.
whether . . . or not	**whether** I locked the door **or not**.
if	I can't remember **if** I locked the door.
if . . . or not	**if** I locked the door **or not**.
Question Clauses	
who, whoever, whom	**Whoever** arrives at the bus station first should buy the tickets.
which, what, where	Do you know **where** the bus station is?
when, why, how	We should ask **when** the bus arrives.
how much, how many	Do not worry about **how much** they cost.
how long, how often, etc.	He didn't care **how long** he had to wait.

Notice that some subordinating conjunctions can introduce different kinds of dependent clauses. *That* can introduce either noun clauses or adjective clauses, and *where* can introduce either a noun, an adjective, or an adverb clause. It normally is not important to know the kind of clause.

> I can't remember **where** I put the house key. (noun clause; direct object of *remember*)

> It's not in the place **where** I usually put it. (adjective clause; tells *which place*)

> I always put it **where** I will see it when I go out the front door. (adverb clause; tells *where I put it*)

C. Conjunctive Adverbs

Conjunctive adverbs can appear at the beginning, in the middle, or at the end of one independent clause, but we often use them to connect two independent clauses.

Remember to put a semicolon before and a comma after the conjunctive adverb if an independent clause follows.

Conjunctive Adverb	Examples
To add a similar idea	
also	Community colleges offer preparation for many jobs; **also,** they prepare students to transfer to four-year colleges or universities.
besides	; **besides,**
furthermore	; **furthermore,**
in addition	; **in addition,**
moreover	; **moreover,**
To add an unexpected or surprising continuation	
however	The cost of attending a community college is low; **however,** many students need financial aid.
nevertheless	; **nevertheless,**
nonetheless	; **nonetheless,**
still	; **still,**
To add a complete contrast	
in contrast	Most community colleges do not have dormitories; **in contrast,** most four-year colleges do.
on the other hand	; **on the other hand,**
To add a result	
as a result	Native and nonnative English speakers have different needs; **as a result,** most schools provide separate classes for each group.
consequently	; **consequently,**
therefore	; **therefore,**
thus	; **thus,**

Appendix 3   Above material from: *Writing Academic English Level 4, Fourth Edition*

To list ideas in order of time	
meanwhile	Police kept people away from the scene of the accident; **meanwhile**, ambulance workers tried to pull victims out of the wreck.
afterward	The workers put five injured people into an ambulance; **afterward**, they found another victim.
then	; **then**,
subsequently	; **subsequently**,

To give an example	
for example	Colors can have different meanings; **for example**, white is the color of weddings in some cultures and of funerals in others.
for instance	; **for instance**,

To show similarities	
similarly	Hawaii has sunshine and friendly people; **similarly**, Mexico's weather is sunny and its people hospitable.
likewise	; **likewise**,

To indicate "the first statement is not true; the second statement is true"	
instead	The medicine did not make him feel better; **instead**, it made him feel worse.
on the contrary	; **on the contrary**,
rather	; **rather**,
instead (meaning "as a substitute")	They had planned to go to Hawaii on their honeymoon; **instead**, they went to Mexico.

To give another possibility	
on the other hand	You can live in a dorm on campus; **on the other hand**, you can rent a room with a family off campus.
alternatively	; **alternatively**,
otherwise (meaning "if not")	Students must take final exams; **otherwise**, they will receive a grade of Incomplete.

To add an explanation	
in other words	Some cultures are matriarchal; **in other words,** the mothers are the head of the family.
that is	; **that is,**
To make a stronger statement	
indeed	Mangoes are a very common fruit; **indeed,** people eat more mangoes than any other fruit in the world.
in fact	; **in fact,**

D. TRANSITION SIGNALS

Transition Signals and Conjunctive Adverbs	Coordinating Conjunctions and Paired Conjunctions	Subordinating Conjunctions	Others: Adjectives, Prepositions, Verbs
To list ideas in order of time			
first, . . . first of all, . . . second, . . . third, . . . next, . . . then . . . after that, . . . meanwhile, . . . in the meantime, . . . finally, . . . last, . . . last of all, . . . subsequently, . . .		before after until when while as soon as since	the first (reason, cause, step, etc.) the second . . . the third . . . another . . . the last . . . the final . . .

Appendix 3   Above material from: *Writing Academic English Level 4, Fourth Edition*

To list ideas in order of importance			
first, . . .			the first . . . (reason, cause, step, etc.)
first of all, . . .			
first and foremost, . . .			an additional . . .
second, . . .			the second . . .
more important, . . .			another . . .
most important, . . .			a more important (reason, cause, step, etc.)
more significantly, . . .			
most significantly, . . .			the most important . . .
above all, . . .			the most significant . . .
most of all, . . .			the best/the worst . . .
To add a similar or equal idea			
also, . . .	and		another . . . (reason, cause, step, etc.)
besides, . . .	both . . . and		a second . . .
furthermore, . . .	not only . . . but also		an additional . . .
in addition, . . .			a final . . .
moreover, . . .			as well as
too			
as well			
To add an opposite idea			
however, . . .	but	although	despite
on the other hand, . . .	yet	even though	in spite of
nevertheless, . . .		though	
nonetheless, . . .			
still, . . .			

To explain or restate an idea			
in other words, . . .			
in particular, . . .			
(more) specifically, . . .			
that is, . . .			
To make a stronger statement			
indeed, . . .			
in fact, . . .			
To give another possibility			
alternatively, . . .	or		
on the other hand, . . .	either . . . or		
otherwise, . . .	whether . . . or		
To give an example			
for example, . . .			such as
for instance, . . .			an example of
			to exemplify
To express an opinion			
according to . . .			to believe (that)
in my opinion, . . .			to feel (that)
in my view, . . .			to think (that)
To give a reason			
for this reason, . . .	for	because	as a result of
			because of
			due to

To give a result			
accordingly, . . . as a consequence, . . . as a result, . . . consequently, . . . for these reasons, . . . hence, . . . therefore, . . . thus, . . .	so		the cause of the reason for to cause to result (in) to have an effect on to affect
To add a conclusion			
all in all, . . . in brief, . . . in short, . . . to conclude, . . . to summarize, . . . in conclusion, . . . in summary, . . . for these reasons, . . .			
To show similarities			
likewise, . . . similarly, . . . also	and both . . . and not only . . . but also neither . . . nor		alike, like, just like as, just as as well as well as compared with or to in comparison with or to to be similar (to) too

To show differences			
however, . . .			instead of
in contrast, . . .			
instead, . . .			
on the contrary, . . .			
on the other hand, . . .			
rather, . . .			

Appendix 4
Punctuation Rules

Using correct punctuation is important because punctuation conveys meaning just as words do. Consider these two sentences:

> Eat children.
> Eat, children.

Both sentences are commands, but the first sentence would be correct only in a society of cannibals[1]! Learn and practice the rules of punctuation until you are confident about using them correctly.

A. COMMAS[2]

Commas are sometimes troublesome to learners of English because they are used differently in other languages. There are many comma rules in English, but you may remember them more easily if you realize that they can be organized into just four main groups: **introducers, coordinators, inserters,** and **tags.** Each group of commas relates to independent clauses in a particular way, except the coordinator group. Coordinator commas link not just independent clauses but *any* coordinate (equal) elements in a sentence.

Study the examples for each comma group, and notice the kinds of elements that can be introducers, coordinators, inserters, and tags.

1. Introducer Commas

An introducer comma follows any element that comes in front of the first independent clause in a sentence.

	Therefore, I plan to quit smoking.
	Nervously, I threw away my cigarettes.
WORDS	**As a result,** I feel terrible right now.
	After 16 years of smoking, it is not easy to quit.
PHRASES	**Having smoked for 16 years,** I find it difficult to quit.

---

[1]*cannibals:* people who eat human flesh
[2]Thanks to Anne Katz of ARC Associates, Oakland, California, for permission to adapt her presentation of comma rules.

DEPENDENT CLAUSES	**Because I have a chronic cough,** my doctor recommended that I quit immediately.
DIRECT QUOTATIONS	**"Stop smoking today,"** she advised.

2. Coordinator Commas

Together with a coordinating conjunction, a comma links coordinate (equal) elements in a sentence.

COMPOUND SENTENCE WITH 2 INDEPENDENT CLAUSES	**She has a good job,** yet **she is always broke.** **They were tired,** so **they went home early.**
SERIES OF 3 OR MORE WORDS	He does not enjoy **skiing, ice-skating,** or **sledding.** Cecille speaks **English, Spanish, French,** and **Creole.** (*No comma with only two items: Chen speaks Mandarin and Taiwanese.*)
SERIES OF 3 OR MORE PHRASES	A nurse has to work **at night, on weekends,** and **on holidays.** We **ran into the airport, checked our luggage, raced to the boarding gate, gave the attendant our boarding passes,** and **collapsed in our seats.**

3. Inserter Commas

An inserter comma is used before and after any element that is inserted into the middle of an independent clause.

WORDS	My uncle, **however,** refuses to quit smoking.
PHRASES	My father, **on the other hand,** has never smoked. There is no point in living, **according to my uncle,** if you do not do what you enjoy.
NONRESTRICTIVE PHRASES AND CLAUSES	My aunt, **his wife,** died of lung cancer. My cousins, **grieving over their mother's death,** resolved never to smoke. My mother, **who just celebrated her fiftieth birthday,** enjoys an occasional cigarette.
REPORTING VERBS IN DIRECT QUOTATIONS	"I have tried to quit dozens of times**," she says,** "but I can't."

4. Tag Commas

A tag comma is used when adding certain elements to the end of a sentence.

WORDS	My uncle believes in drinking a daily glass of wine, **too.**[3] He appears to be in good health, **however.**
PHRASES	He swims for an hour every day, **for example.** He also plays tennis, **beating me most of the time.**
TAG QUESTIONS	It is not logical, **is it**?
DIRECT QUOTATIONS	He laughs as he says, **"I will outlive all of you."**

[3]Many writers do not use a comma before *too*.

Appendix 4   Above material from: *Writing Academic English Level 4, Fourth Edition*

B. Practice 1: Using Commas

Step 1

Add commas wherever they are necessary. (Not all sentences need them, and some sentences need more than one.)

Step 2

Name the function of each comma (introducer, coordinator, inserter, or tag) on the line.

The first one has been done for you as an example.

1. *Inserter* The advertising industry, which is one of the largest industries in the United States, employs millions of people and spends billions of dollars.

2. _____ A company that wants to be successful must spend a great deal of money to advertise its products.

3. _____ Advertising is essential to the free enterprise system yet it can sometimes be very annoying.

4. _____ Every minute of the day and night people are exposed to ads on television on billboards in the newspapers and in magazines.

5. _____ You cannot even avoid advertising in the privacy of your own car or your own home for advertisers have begun selling their products in those places too.

6. _____ In the last few years advertising agencies have started to hire young people to hand out circulars on street corners and in parking lots.

7. _____ You can often find these circulars stuck on your windshield thrust through the open windows of your car stuffed in your mailbox or simply scattered on your front doorstep.

8. _____ Because Americans are exposed to so much advertising they have become immune to it.

9. _____ As a result advertisers have to make louder commercials use brighter colors and hire sexier models to catch the public's attention.

10. _____ Many people object to commercials that use sex as a sales strategy.

11. _____ Sexy commercials that sell everything from toothpaste to automobiles seem to imply that you will become sexier if you buy the product.

12. _____ Sex is used in many cigarette and liquor ads for example.

13. _____ The women in such ads are often dressed in revealing clothes and are surrounded by handsome men and the men in such ads are always extremely handsome and virile.

14. _____ As everyone knows smoking and drinking do not make you sexy or virile.

15. _____ On the contrary drinking makes you fat and smoking makes you sick.

16. _____ Recently smoking was banned in most public places in the United States.

17. _____ Many people opposed the law but it finally passed.

18. _____ Smoking is now prohibited in hospitals airports stores offices and restaurants.

19. _____ In many other countries however smoking is still allowed.

20. _____ Antismoking groups want to ban smoking in those countries too.

C. SEMICOLONS

Using **semicolons** is not difficult if you remember that a semicolon (;) is more like a period than a comma. It is a very strong punctuation mark. Semicolons are used in three places:

1. Between two sentences that are closely connected in idea

2. Before conjunctive adverbs and some transition phrases when they are followed by an independent clause

3. Between items in a series when the items themselves contain commas

1. Between Sentences

Use a semicolon at the end of a sentence when the following sentence is closely connected in meaning. You could also use a period, but when the sentences are connected in meaning, a semicolon indicates the connection.

Independent clause; independent clause.
Andrew did not accept the job offer; he wants to go to graduate school.
Computer use is increasing; computer crime is, too.
The meeting ended at dawn; nothing had been decided.

2. Before Connectors

Use a semicolon before conjunctive adverbs such as *however, therefore, nevertheless, moreover,* and *furthermore.* Also use a semicolon before transition phrases such as *for example, as a result, that is,* or *in fact* when they are followed by an independent clause.

	conjunctive adverb,	
Independent clause;	OR	**independent clause.**
	transition phrase,	

Skiing is dangerous; nevertheless, millions of people ski.
I have never been to Asia; in fact, I have never been outside the country.

3. Between Items in a Series

Semicolons are used to separate items in a series when some of the items already contain commas.

I cannot decide which car I like best: the Ferrari, with its quick acceleration and sporty look; the midsize Ford Taurus, with its comfortable seats and ease of handling; or the compact Geo, with its economical fuel consumption.

D. Practice 2: Using Semicolons and Commas

A. **Step 1** The following sentences need semicolons; some also need commas. Add the correct punctuation in the appropriate places.

Step 2 On the line at the left, indicate whether the semicolon is

1. before two closely connected sentences.
2. before a conjunctive adverb or a transition phrase.
3. between items in a series if the items already contain commas.

The first one is done for you as an example.

1. ___2___ Professor Smith is at a conference; however, Dr. Jones, who is the department chairman, will be glad to see you.

2. _____ Grace works for a prestigious law firm she is their top criminal lawyer.

3. _____ My favorite leisure-time activities are going to movies especially musicals reading novels especially stories of love and adventure listening to music both rock and classical and participating in sports particularly tennis and volleyball.

4. _____ The future of our wild animals is uncertain for example illegal shooting and chemical poisoning threaten many birds.

5. _____ Homework is boring therefore I never do it.

6. _____ The freeways are always crowded during the busy rush hours nevertheless people refuse to take public transportation.

7. _____ The Smiths' marriage should succeed they share the same interests.

8. _____ Hoping that he would pass the course he stayed up all night studying for the final exam unfortunately he overslept and missed the test.

9. _____ In general I enjoy my English class the amount of homework our teacher assigns is definitely not enjoyable however.

10. _____ If you are a college student, an average day is filled with challenges: you have to avoid running into Professor Jones whose class you missed because you overslept you have to race across the campus at high speed to reach your next class which is always at the other side of the campus and you have to secretly prepare your homework assignment during class hoping all the time that the teacher will not catch you.

B. Punctuate the following sentences by adding semicolons and commas. Use semicolons wherever possible.

1. My bus was late therefore I missed my first class.

2. The politician was discovered accepting bribes as a result his political career was ruined.

3. My father never cries in fact he never shows any emotion at all,

4. The restaurant was closed consequently we went home to eat.

5. Some people feel that grades are unnecessary on the other hand some people feel that grades motivate students.

6. Technology is changing our lives in harmful ways for example the computer is replacing human contact.

7. The computer dehumanizes business nevertheless it has some real advantages,

8. Writing essays is easy it just takes a little practice.

9. North Americans love pets every family seems to have at least one dog or cat.

10. The life expectancy of North Americans is increasing for example the life expectancy of a person born in 2000 was 77.2 years which is an increase of almost 30 years since 1900.

11. Your proposal is a good one however I do not completely agree with your final suggestion.

12. Efficiency is a highly prized quality among North Americans it has almost attained the status of a moral attribute.

C. Write one original sentence for each of the three rules for using semicolons.

1. Between closely connected sentences

_____

2. Before conjunctive adverbs and some transition phrases

_____

3. Between items in a series

_____

E. COLONS

Using a **colon** at the end of an independent clause focuses attention on the words following the colon. After a colon, we often write lists, appositives, and direct quotations.

1. Before Lists

Use a colon to introduce a list.

Libraries have two kinds of periodicals: bound periodicals and current periodicals.

I need the following groceries: eggs, milk, and coffee.

The causes of the U.S. Civil War were as follows: the economic domination of the North, the slavery issue, and the issue of states' rights versus federal intervention.

2. Caution

1. Do not use a colon to introduce a list after the verb *to be* unless you add *the following* or *as follows*.

INCORRECT   To me, the most important things in life are: good health, a happy home life, and a satisfying occupation.

CORRECT   To me, the most important things in life **are** good health, a happy home life, and a satisfying occupation.

CORRECT   To me, the most important things in life **are the following:** good health, a happy home life, and a satisfying occupation.

Appendix 4   Above material from: *Writing Academic English Level 4, Fourth Edition*

INCORRECT   2. Do not use a colon after a preposition. Use a colon only at the end of an independent clause.

CORRECT   After a long day at work, I look forward to: enjoying a quiet dinner at home, playing with my children, and watching a little TV.

After a long day at work, I look forward to enjoying a quiet dinner at home, playing with my children, and watching a little TV.

3. Before Appositives

Use a colon after an independent clause to direct attention to an appositive (a word or word group that renames another word or word group).

He had one great love in his life: himself.

A doctor has two important abilities: the ability to listen and the ability to analyze.

4. Before Long Quotations

Use a colon to introduce a quotation longer than three lines. This type of quote is indented on both sides, and no quotation marks are used.

As Albert C. Baugh and Thomas Cable state in their book *The History of the English Language*:

There is no such thing as uniformity in language. Not only does the speech of one community differ from that of another, but the speech of different individuals of a single community, even different members of the same family, is marked by individual peculiarities.

5. Before Subtitles

Use a colon between the main title and the subtitle of a book, article, or play.

A popular book on nonverbal communication is Samovar and Porter's *Intercultural Communication: A Reader*.

The title of an article from the *New York Times* is "Man on Mars: Dream or Reality?"

6. In Expressions of Time or Day

Use a colon between the numbers for hours and minutes when indicating the time of day.

Helen left the class at 12:30.

Their plane arrived at 1:40 A.M., six hours late.

7. After Formal Salutations

Use a colon after the salutation of a formal letter.

Dear Professor Einstein:

Dear Customer Relations:

Dear Ms. Smith:

To Whom It May Concern:

In informal letters, use a comma.

Dear Mom,

Dear Mark,

F. Practice 3: Using Punctuation Marks

A. Add commas, semicolons, and colons to the following.

1. The library offers many special services the Student Learning Center where students can receive individual tutoring special classes where they can improve their math reading writing and computer skills and group study rooms where they can meet with classmates to discuss assignments.

2. Dear Dr. Patterson

   Dear Jacob

   Dear Mr. Carter

3. To check a book out of the library you should follow this procedure Write down the call number of the book find the book take it to the circulation desk fill out the card and show your student I.D.

4. The principal sources of air pollution in our cities are factories airplanes and automobiles.

5. I have a dental appointment at 330 today. Please pick me up at 300.

B. Write a sentence in which you list two pieces of advice that you have received from someone older, such as your parents or a teacher. Use a colon to direct attention to them.

_____

_____

C. Write the title and subtitle of the following book correctly. Remember to underline the full title.

TITLE	SUBTITLE
Paris	A Visitor's Guide to Restaurants

G. Quotation Marks

Quotation marks ("...") have three basic uses: to enclose direct quotations, to enclose unusual words, and to enclose titles of short works.

1. Around Direct Quotations

Use quotation marks around a direct quotation that is shorter than three lines. A direct quotation states the *exact* words of a speaker and is usually introduced by a reporting phrase such as *he said* or *as the report stated*.

Punctuation with quotation marks can be a little tricky. Here are some rules to follow:

1. Separate a quoted sentence from a reporting phrase with a comma.

   The receptionist said**,** "The doctor is unavailable right now. Please wait."

   "We have already been waiting for an hour**,**" we answered.

2. Periods and commas go inside the second quotation mark of a pair.

   "I thought he was responsible**,**" he said, "but he isn't**.**"

3. Colons and semicolons go outside quotation marks.

   "Give me liberty or give me death"**:** these are famous words.

4. Exclamation points (!) and question marks (?) go inside quotation marks if they are a part of the quotation; otherwise, they go outside.

   "Is it eight o'clock**?**" she asked.

   Did she say, "It is eight o'clock"**?**

5. Begin each quoted sentence with a capital letter. When a quoted sentence is divided into two parts, the second part begins with a lowercase letter unless it is a new sentence.

   "**I** thought he was responsible," he said, "**b**ut he isn't."

   "**I** think he is responsible," he said. "**L**ook at his fine work."

6. Use single quotation marks ('. . .') to enclose a quotation within a quotation.

   As John F. Kennedy reminded us, "We should never forget the words of Martin Luther King, Jr., who said, **'**I have a dream.**'** "

2. Around Unusual Words

Use quotation marks around words with an unusual, especially ironic, meanings.

   The **"banquet"** consisted of hot dogs and soft drinks.

   The little girl proudly showed her **"masterpiece"**: a crayon drawing of a flower.

3. Around Titles of Short Works

Use quotation marks around the titles of articles from periodical journals, magazines, and newspapers; chapters of books; short stories; poems; and songs.

   In the article **"The Future of Manned Space Travel,"** published in the July 19, 2004, issue of *Space*, the authors explore the problems of a manned flight to Mars.

   The *Times* of London recently published an article entitled **"Who Needs the Monarchy?"** in which the relevancy of the English monarchy was discussed.

Note: Underline or *italicize* titles of books, journals, magazines, newspapers, and movies.

H. Practice 4: Using Quotation Marks

Write five sentences about any article in a newspaper or magazine that you enjoy reading. Include a quotation, the name of the newspaper or magazine, and the title of the article in each sentence.

I. Editing Practice

Add punctuation to the following paragraphs.

Aging

1   [1]People are more likely to live long enough to get old in wealthy countries than in poor countries. [2]In rich countries people have nutritious food modern medical care good sanitation and clean drinking water but poor countries lack these things. [3]As a result the mortality rate especially infant mortality is very high. [4]Citizens of Ethiopia and Yemen which are two of the world's poorest countries have an average life expectancy of 35–39 years. [5]Citizens of Japan Hong Kong Singapore Australia

Iceland and Sweden in contrast have an average life span of more than 80 years. [6]Japan has the highest Yemen has the lowest. [7]One exception is Saudi Arabia one of the world's wealthiest nations. [8]Having an average life expectancy of 45–49 years Saudi Arabians live about as long as Bangladeshis and Cambodians. [9]Surprisingly the United States is not among the highest rated nations having an average life expectancy of only 77 years.

2   [10]Compared to other mammals humans have a relatively long life span. [11]The average life span of elephants is 70 years of dogs 18 years of cats 14 years and of horses 20 years. [12]The life spans of other species are as follows eagles parrots and owls 60 years parakeets 12 years guppies 5 years and box tortoises 100 years. [13]Some plants such as trees live much longer than animals. [14]Redwood trees for example live more than 3,000 years and bristlecone pine trees can live over 4,000 years.

3   [15]The life expectancy of people who live in industrialized societies is increasing rapidly in fact it has doubled in the past hundred years. [16]When comparing males and females one finds that women generally live longer than men. [17]The oldest person in the world until recently was a French woman Jeanne Calment. [18]At her death Madame Calment was both blind and deaf but had not lost her sharp wit for which she had become quite famous. [19]Asked what kind of future she expected she replied A very short one. [20]Bragging about her smooth skin she said I've only had one wrinkle in my life and I'm sitting on it.

109 Target Achievement Goals (TAGs)

It is essential for you to write well in English. So, we have set **T**arget **A**chievement **G**oals—**TAGs**—which are important objectives for your writing. We are focusing on the basics so that everyone will understand your writing. At ELS, you will work on your writing skills, using the TAGs to write good, clear, accurate sentences. Use these TAGs every time you write, and your writing will improve.

We want you to pay attention to these details in particular:

- **TAG 1—The Topic:** *Your writing assignment has to address the topic*—this means that you must be sure that you write about the topic that your teacher gives you. If your writing does not address the topic, you will not meet your TAG.

- **TAG 2—Subjects and Verbs:** *All of your sentences must have subjects and verbs.* **Check your sentences for missing verbs or subjects.** *If you have 2 sentences missing verbs, or two sentences missing subjects, or one of each, you will not meet your TAG. If you have the* same mistake many times, your teacher will count it as *a different mistake* each time.

  Wrong: He a doctor. (missing verb) **Right:** He <u>is</u> a doctor.
  Wrong: Is a book on the table. (missing subject) **Right:** <u>There</u> is a book on the table.

- **TAG 3—Verb Tenses:** *All of your sentences must use the correct tenses in the correct forms.* **Check every verb in every sentence.** *If you have 2 sentences with incorrect tenses or incorrect forms, you will not meet your TAG.* If you have the same mistake many times, your teacher will count it as *a different mistake* each time. As a 109 student, you are responsible for **all** of the major tenses.

  Wrong: I shop for clothes yesterday. (wrong tense) **Right:** I <u>shopped</u> for clothes yesterday.
  Wrong: John going to Denver. (incomplete tense form) **Right:** John <u>is going</u> to Denver.

- **TAG 4—Word Order:** *All of your sentences must have the correct word order.* **Check every sentence for word order.** *If you have 2 sentences with mistakes in word order—statements, questions, or negatives—you will not meet your TAG.* If you have the same mistake many times, your teacher will count it as *a different mistake* each time.

  Wrong: She studied her lessons last night at home hard. (statement) **Right:** She studied her lessons <u>hard at home last night</u>.
  Standard Statement Word Order:
  Subject+Verb+Object+Manner Adverb+Place Adverb+Time Adverb

Wrong: Did Tom mailed the letter? (question) **Right:** Did Tom <u>mail</u> the letter?
Standard Question Word Order:

Operator+Subject+Base Form of Verb+Object+Manner Adverb+Place
Adverb+Time Adverb

Wrong: I no have my pencil today. (negative) **Right:** I <u>don't</u> have my pencil today.
Standard Negative Statement Word Order:

Subject+Negative Operator+Base Form of Verb+Object+Manner Adverb+Place
Adverb+Time Adverb

- **TAG 5—Capitalization and Punctuation:** *The first word of all of your sentences must begin with a capital letter. Proper nouns should be capitalized. Use correct punctuation at the end of your sentences—commas, semicolons, and colons.* **Check all of your sentences for capitalization and punctuation.** *If you have 3 errors in capitalization and/or punctuation you will not meet your TAG. If you have the same mistake many times, your teacher will count it as <u>a different mistake</u> each time.*

  Wrong: the house is red (beginning capital; final period) **Right:** The house is red.
  Wrong: robert and i fish in lake como (capitalize names of specific people and places; capitalize "I"; use final punctuation) **Right:** Robert and I fish in Lake Como.

- **TAG 6—Spelling:** *You must spell all of the words on the list of the 500 Most Common Words for Spelling correctly.* **Check your spelling; use the list.** *If you have 3 mistakes in spelling any of the 500 words, you will not meet your TAG. If you have the same mistake many times, your teacher will count it as* <u>a different mistake</u> *each time.*

  Wrong: Meny people know wear I live. **Right:** <u>Many</u> people know <u>where</u> I live.

For Your Regular Classroom Assignments

If your paper *meets* all of your TAGs:

- Your teacher will correct it, grade it and give it back to you.
- You can rewrite it in class.
- After you rewrite your paper, you will give it back to the teacher with the original by the next class.
- You can receive up to 5 more points on your writing assignment grade for your revision.
- **You <u>must</u> revise your writing assignment. If you do not revise your paper, your grade for the entire writing assignment will be 0.**

If your paper *does not meet* one or more of your TAGs:

- **Your teacher will stop reading.**
- **Your paper will <u>fail</u>,** *but* **you will have one chance to correct it.**
- Your teacher will show you your mistakes so that **you can fix your paper**.
- You **have to** fix your paper the **same** day the teacher gives it back to you.
- **You may <u>not</u> take your paper home.**
- Fix the mistakes your teacher showed you by rewriting the problem sentences correctly. **You can completely rewrite your paper <u>only</u> if your teacher tells you that you did not address the topic.**
- Your teacher will tell you when and where you can fix your paper.
- After you fix your paper, give it back to the teacher.
- If you reach your TAGs after you fix your mistakes, the teacher will correct and grade your paper.

Appendix 5 Above material from: *ELS Language Centers*

- The teacher will give it back to you to rewrite.
- After you rewrite your paper, you will give it back to the teacher with the original by the next class.
- **You <u>must</u> revise your writing assignment. If you do not revise your paper, your grade for the entire writing assignment will be 0. If you did not reach your TAGs the first time, you are not eligible for the additional 5 points.**
- **If you do not reach your TAGs after you fix your mistakes, your paper will fail.**

For Your Final Writing Exam

If your paper meets all of your TAGs, your teacher will

- grade your exam.
- **not correct it.**
- tell you what your final exam grade is for your writing test, but will not give you back your paper to keep.
- give you the writing rubrics form for your writing exam, which will show where your strengths and weaknesses are.
- make comments on the writing rubrics form about how you can improve your writing.
- discuss your writing exam with you during the last class of the session.

If your paper does not meet any <u>one</u> of your TAGs

- **Your teacher will stop reading.**
- Your paper will **fail**.
- There will be **no** chance to fix it.
- You will fail the exam.
- You will fail your Writing course.
- Your overall grade for your Writing course will be 0.5.
- You will repeat the level.
- Your teacher will give you the writing rubric form for your writing exam, which shows which TAGs you did not reach.
- Your teacher will discuss your paper with you during the last class of the session.

If you have any questions about this, talk to the teacher any time during the course and before the final exam; he or she will be happy to help you.

LEVEL 107 WRITING EVALUATION

Teacher: _____ Date: _____ Student: _____

☐ Addresses topic

☐ Does not address topic

	Above standard	Standard	Below standard	Unsatisfactory	Teacher comments
Grammatical accuracy	30 **Accurate control of all structures** used for time and voice. No errors with prepositions. Several examples of good, accurate use of sophisticated structures.	24 Sentence form is accurate and varied for time and voice. Good **attempts at more sophisticated structures.** Incorporates both coordination and subordination. Limited but repeated errors based on L1 (e.g. missing articles).	21 **Some sentences have grammatical problems** (based on level 7 grammar knowledge), but there is evidence of knowledge of structures taught. Errors never affect comprehension.	0 **Errors occur that confuse the meaning of sentences.** OR, may have run on sentences. May use complex forms but evidence of underlying basic errors.	
Vocabulary/ Spelling	20 Broad vocabulary allows for **detailed exploration** of the topic with few wrong choices. Appropriate use of adjectives and adverbs. No spelling problems.	16 Vocabulary **sufficient for full examination** of topic with few poor choices. Adjectives and adverbs used effectively. Only minor spelling problems with less frequently used words.	12 Full examination of the topic but **areas of weakness** due to vocabulary limitations. All sentences are easy to understand. Fewer than 1 spelling mistake per sentence and only with less frequently used words.	0 **Difficult to understand** due to vocabulary errors. Thesis cannot be clearly defended due to vocabulary limitations. May have frequent bad choices or misspellings.	
Length/Format	13 4-5 paragraph essay of more than 325 words, sufficient length to allow for ample exploration of supporting ideas.	10 4-5 paragraph essay of more than 225 words. Paragraphs are of a sufficient length to allow for adequate exploration of supporting ideas.	9 4-5 paragraph essay between 175 and 225 words. OR, fewer than 5 paragraphs, inadequate for exploration of supporting ideas.	0 Fewer than 175 words. OR, did not use correct paragraphing format.	
Introduction/ Thesis statement	12 Introduction is **well crafted,** and provides ample background—leads directly to the thesis statement. Thesis is clear, concise, and presents a basis for all of the main points of the essay.	10 Introduction provides background leading to the thesis. The thesis is a clear statement. Although both intro and thesis are **well constructed, they are basic.**	8 Introduction is too **simplistic** and does not build directly to the thesis. OR, thesis statement not targeted accurately to topic.	0 **No** introduction or no thesis. OR, thesis is unrelated to essay, OR, thesis is not clear—too general or too specific.	
Organization/ Development	13 Topic is fully developed with **well-chosen examples** and evidence. Obvious flow in each paragraph and between paragraphs. Idea builds towards the conclusion. Signal words and related punctuation are correctly and effectively used to direct relations between ideas.	10 Topic is developed over several paragraphs. Each paragraph has a controlling topic sentence and **adequate** supporting evidence. Each paragraph logically transitions to the next paragraph. Signal words and related punctuation are used correctly.	8 May have limited development due to **one or two poorly chosen examples.** Some attempts to use organization in and between paragraphs. Some signal words are used to control flow of ideas.	0 **Limited development** of idea due to overall weak exploration of examples or evidence. Although there may be attempts at internal organization, it is not consistent. May have poor choices of signal words.	
Conclusion	12 Conclusion fully summarizes all the points of the essay. It extends **beyond just a repeat of the thesis.**	10 Conclusion is **logical and comprehensive.** It summarizes all of the main points presented in the body	8 Conclusion is **too short** or introduces extraneous information.	0 **No,** or very limited, attempt at a conclusion.	

Total points: _____/100   Teacher's Initials: _____

Revision/2nd draft: _____/100 (up to 5 points; not for final exam)

LEVEL 108 WRITING EVALUATION   Teacher: Date: Student:

☐ Addresses topic   ☐ Does not address topic

	Above standard	Standard	Below standard	Unsatisfactory	Teacher comments
Grammatical accuracy	30 **No serious grammatical errors.** Sentence structures are varied. Uses advanced signal words with ease and without error. No errors with articles or punctuation.	24 **Basic sentence forms are controlled,** although there may be problems due to complexity of the structures. At least 2 correct uses of complex sentence structures. Signal words are used with appropriate punctuation. May have limited but repeated errors based on L1 (e.g. missing articles).	21 **Occasional errors** with complex structures such as subordination. Errors with compound/complex sentence structures. Uses basic signal words. Occasional errors with high frequency punctuation and articles. No sentence has more than one grammatical error (based on level 8 standards).	0 May have run-on sentences. Does not attempt complex grammatical structures such as subordination. **Consists mostly of short, simple sentences.** May have one or more sentences that are incomprehensible.	
Vocabulary	20 Vocabulary is varied and offers a **robust exploration of the topic.** Use of adjectives and adverbs adds detail and complexity to the writing. No spelling mistakes.	16 Vocabulary is **appropriate** to the topic. Spelling mistakes are limited to low frequency words.	12 Topic development is limited by **lack of advanced vocabulary.** Frequent errors with word form or meaning. All sentences are comprehensible. Spelling mistakes are fewer than 1 per sentence, and only low frequency words.	0 Topic development is very limited with **no use of vocabulary beyond the intermediate level.** May have multiple examples of spelling errors of high-frequency words.	
Length/Format	13 More than 325 words. Uses 4-5 paragraph format. Paragraphs are of a sufficient length to allow for **ample exploration** of supporting ideas.	10 More than 250 words. Uses 4-5 paragraph format. Paragraphs are of a sufficient length to allow for **adequate exploration** of supporting ideas.	9 More than 200 words on an assigned topic. OR, uses 4-5 paragraph format but **some paragraphs consist of three- and four-sentences.**	0 Fewer than 200 words. OR, does not use 5-paragraph format. OR, essay consists only of short, **mostly three-sentence paragraphs.**	
Introduction/Thesis	12 Introduction leads clearly to thesis. Thesis statement is **clear, focused and engages the reader.** It does not rely on formulaic expressions (e.g. "There are three differences . . .). Summarizes the main points of the essay.	10 Good introduction that clearly points to thesis. Clear, well constructed, thesis statement. May **be overly comprehensive or expressed awkwardly.**	8 Uses an introduction. One sentence can be identified as a thesis sentence, but may be **simplistic,** may lack clarity, or may be 2 sentences.	0 May not have an introduction. **No sentence can be identified** as a thesis sentence. OR, thesis statement does not relate to the ideas expressed in the body of the essay.	
Organization/Development	13 Topic is fully explored with **well chosen supporting examples.** A variety of methods of support are used (facts, examples, descriptions, etc.). Paragraphs are constructed to flow to the conclusion. The essay shows evidence of planning and a pattern of organization. Uses introductory phrases and clauses, rather than single words, to transition between paragraphs. All ideas are completely developed.	10 The topic is fully explored. Each paragraph has **sufficient supporting examples.** Paragraphs flow and develop topic step by step. A topic sentence is used in each supporting paragraph. Development leads to conclusion. Uses appropriate transitions between paragraphs.	8 The topic is adequately explored, but **one area is underdeveloped due to weak support** or is left unexplored. OR, although paragraphs are well constructed using topic sentences and examples, the essay may not follow a consistent pattern of organization, making it confusing. Use of transitions, if any, is limited only to the most basic (e.g. first, next, another, etc.)	0 Overall **topic exploration is limited due to weak or under-explored examples.** OR, supporting sentences are short and may be either unrelated to the topic or simply a restatement of the topic sentence. OR, there is no overall control of the essay organization making it very difficult to follow the theme.	
Conclusion	12 The conclusion goes beyond a summary of the essay and offers **a thoughtful exploration** of implications of the topic, future benefits/problems, or offers solutions.	10 The conclusion is **logical and comprehensive.** It summarizes the majority of the main points presented in the body and offers a final perspective on the topic.	8 **Attempts** to summarize most of the main points of the essay, but misses many. OR, conclusion is simply a restatement of the thesis or the main ideas of the essay.	0 Essay **lacks a conclusion,** or the conclusion consists only of one or two sentences.	

Total points: _____ /100   **Teacher's Initials:** _____   **Revision/2nd draft:** _____ /100 (up to 5 points; not for final exam)

Above material from: *ELS Language Centers*

LEVEL 109 WRITING EVALUATION

Teacher: Date: Student:

☐ Addresses topic   ☐ Does not address topic

☐ Meets TAGs   ☐ Does not meet TAGs because of ☐ 2x missing subject/verb ☐ 2x verb tense ☐ 2x sentence pattern ☐ 3x cap/punct ☐ 3x spell-500

	Above standard	Standard	Below standard	Unsatisfactory	Teacher comments
Grammatical accuracy	30 — Combines several ideas in a sentence and can make use of multiple layers in one sentence. Sentences are **easy to read**. No problems with multiple verb forms in a sentence or within a paragraph.	24 — Firm control of most grammatical forms. At least 2 examples of complex sentence structures. Sentences are varied for effect making use of subordination. **Errors are few and result from complexity of structures.** May have limited but repeated errors based on L1 (missing articles).	21 — Demonstrates control of most grammatical forms, but **no examples of complex structures.** Sentences are varied for effect with some use of making subordination. Errors are few and result from complexity of structures.	0 — **No mastery of subordination and may have over-use of coordination.** There may be frequent run-on sentences. Numerous errors in basic grammatical forms and/or simplistic.	
Vocabulary/ Spelling	20 — Uses highly advanced level vocabulary **creatively and accurately** to explore the topic. Adjectives and adverbs add detail and complexity to the writing. No spelling mistakes.	16 — Uses a wide range of vocabulary that allows for **sufficient examples** to develop topic. No spelling mistakes other than infrequently used words that do not follow standard patterns.	12 — Problems with word choice limit **development** of one segment of the essay. All sentences are comprehensible. Fewer than one spelling error per sentence and only infrequently used words.	0 — **Problems with word choice** limit clarity and exploration of several sections of the essay. OR may have an over abundance of spelling mistakes.	
Length/ Format	13 — More than 400 words and will use correct 4–5-paragraph format. Paragraphs are of a sufficient length to allow for **ample exploration of supporting ideas.**	10 — More than 300 word essay on the assigned topic. Uses 4–5 paragraph format. Paragraphs are of a sufficient length to allow for **adequate exploration** of supporting ideas. (Generally more than 3 supporting sentences.)	9 — Fewer than 300 words but more than 200, and still in the 4–5 paragraph format. Has **one area in need of further exploration.**	0 — Fewer than 200 words. **Does not fully address topic.** OR, does not use correct paragraphing format.	
Introduction/ Thesis Statement	12 — Well-constructed introduction that sets up the thesis. Thesis statement **sparks interest** and is methodically supported in the essay.	10 — Good introduction that clearly points to thesis. **Comprehensive,** well constructed thesis statement that leads to the key points developed in the essay.	8 — Uses an introduction. One sentence can be identified as a thesis sentence, but may be **simplistic,** may lack clarity, or may be 2 sentences.	0 — May not have an introduction. **No** thesis statement or a thesis that is unrelated to the rest of the essay.	
Organization/ Development	13 — **Well thought out** development. Each point will be well explored with sufficient supporting details and examples. Topic is explored from multiple directions.	10 — Develops **several supporting ideas** that are related to the thesis. Internal organization is clear. The topic is clarified and advanced using transition words.	8 — Body of essay is clear in its purpose but at least **one area suffers from lack of development** of ideas.	0 — **Little to no development** beyond a skeletal analysis. May have confusing development that is highly repetitive and does not progress beyond the introduction.	
Conclusion	12 — A valid, supported, **fully developed conclusion** that summarizes all evidence presented in the body. Goes beyond a summary of the essay.	10 — **Fully developed** conclusion that ties up all of the important points.	8 — Conclusion is a **simple** repetition of the basic points of the essay.	0 — **The conclusion is not related** to the essay (introduces new ideas unrelated to or not mentioned in the essay). OR, the essay has **no** conclusion or a conclusion that is not understandable.	

Total points: _____/100   Teacher's Initials: _____   Revision/2nd draft: _____/100 (up to 5 points; not for final exam)

Above material from: *ELS Language Centers*